JUST CHECKING SCORES

TV Anchor Publicly Shamed by Husband's Secret Life

MARISA BURKE

Black Rose Writing | Texas

First printing

Some names and identifying details have been changed to protect the privacy of individuals.

ISBN: 978-1-68433-835-1
PUBLISHED BY BLACK ROSE WRITING
www.blackrosewriting.com

Printed in the United States of America
Suggested Retail Price (SRP) $19.95

Just Checking Scores is printed in Garamond

*As a planet-friendly publisher, Black Rose Writing does its best to eliminate unnecessary waste to reduce paper usage and energy costs, while never compromising the reading experience. As a result, the final word count vs. page count may not meet common expectations.

I dedicate this book to my children, Rachael and Sarah, who persevered through it all.

JUST CHECKING SCORES

PROLOGUE

Eyes glued to computer monitors. Constant click of fingers on keyboards. The steady ding of email notifications. Phones ringing and vibrating. Staccato beat of conversations. An invisible line of energy, taut with anticipation, connecting it all. This is what a typical election day is like in a television newsroom. But, the day before is often just a regular news day, not really thinking ahead, but staying focused on the current day's news.

November 5, 2012 was no different at Channel 16, WNEP-TV, the ABC affiliate in Wilkes-Barre/Scranton, Pennsylvania where I had been working as a broadcast journalist since 1984. My current role was news producer and lead anchor of our top-rated 6 p.m. newscast. I was also the solo anchor of the noon newscast, another show with an enormous audience. It was a balancing act, but I loved every second of it. I never grew tired of the rush of gathering facts, putting them together, and sharing the stories on-air.

I have to admit, election coverage wasn't my favorite. I always felt uneasy approaching election days. While I always focused on delivering accurate facts in all my reporting, there was something a bit more stressful about election results. I worried about saying everything just right. I'm sure that was somewhere in the back of my mind, but I remember it being a routine news day. I don't remember any breaking news. So, I was calm coming off the set after anchoring the noon news, focused on finishing my responsibilities for that day, not the next.

The news I was about to receive, though, had nothing to do with elections, national or world stories, or local news – not yet – but it would change my life forever.

The newsroom in the middle of a regular day is somewhat quiet, and this was the case on that November day in 2012. Reporters and photographers were out gathering news. The assignment editors, and news producers and directors were the only people in the newsroom. It was missing the late-afternoon energy when everyone is back from the field, looking at the clock as a tight deadline looms. I walked back to my desk in the newsroom, which was a maze of cubicles separated by partitions that were only about chest high. The assignment desk was elevated above us all. So, the environment fostered yelling over to a colleague to ask a question about an upcoming story. It didn't provide a whole lot of privacy for phone calls.

I stood in front of my desk as I checked my phone. I had a voicemail from my neighbor who lived across the street. I thought that was strange. He never calls me, let alone, leaves a voicemail.

As I listened to the message, my stomach felt like an elevator in a free-fall.

"Marisa, it's Art. I'm not sure if you know this or not, but the police have your home surrounded. I see state police, local police, and it looks like FBI agents are trying to bust in your front door."

My heartbeat quickened. My mouth went dry. Blood whooshed in my ears. My legs felt wiggly, and my stomach did a few back flips. I steadied myself against my desk. *Not again,* I thought. But, I sensed a tornado in the distance moving as fast and loud as a freight train. And I was in its direct path.

CHAPTER 1

During my senior year of high school, I caught the bug for communications and journalism while serving as the editor of my school's newspaper. After graduation, I attended Cedar Crest College in Allentown, Pennsylvania, a small, all-women's school at that time. I majored in communications and dreamed about writing for a newspaper someday. But then I took a broadcasting course that changed my career path. I wanted to finish my degree at a school with a more established communications program, so I transferred to the Roy H. Park School of Communications at Ithaca College in upstate New York.

I often found it strange that I became a television anchorwoman because, as a child, I was shy. I dreaded every time my mom pulled out the Kodak Instamatic camera—so much so that many times I broke out in tears. To this day, I don't understand why. Maybe it was those weird flash cubes.

I was that kid who always worried about having just the right answer, who never raised my hand, and who got upset if a teacher called on me. I never wanted "all eyes on me." The newspaper route I shared with my younger brother Tim when I was 12 brought me out of my shyness shell. Every Saturday, we went door-to-door to collect money. Tim would finish his route and collections in 30 minutes. It would take me an hour and a half because I was striking up conversations with all my newspaper customers. Then, when I was 15, I started working as a waitress at a restaurant right off Interstate 80 not far from my hometown of Danville, PA. Since it was near a major highway, and I knew the customers were probably traveling somewhere, I always asked my guests questions like where are you from? Where are you heading? I guess even back then, I was curious about people and wanted to hear their stories.

These first jobs helped me overcome my shyness and instilled a strong work ethic, which was also nurtured by my parents, and something I definitely carried into my career as a broadcast journalist.

■   ■   ■

Staying with the same employer for over 30 years is rare these days, even more so when you work in broadcast journalism and at a local television affiliate. So, I knew how lucky I was to have had a career at WNEP-TV Channel 16 that spanned more than three decades. I certainly never would have imagined that happening when, thanks to a close college friend who put in a good word for me with her news director, I landed my first television news job at WSLS-TV in Roanoke, Virginia three months after graduating from Ithaca in 1982.

I envisioned hop-scotching my way across the country as I worked my way up through the television news ranks. I think every broadcast journalist dreams of working in a major, top-20 market. And I did have dreams of working in Philadelphia, but it was more like a fantasy. My real dream was to work at WNEP. I knew how respected the station was; knew it was a news leader, one of the best in the country. That's where I wanted to be.

And it was home. I grew up in Danville, a small borough about 60 miles west of Wilkes-Barre/Scranton, but still within the WNEP viewing area. I wanted to eventually go back home and knew Roanoke was a pit stop on the route to get there.

I was thrilled when I received the letter confirming my position at WSLS-TV. My hard work in school had paid off. I was on my way, but my elation came to a screeching halt after I handed the letter to my parents.

"Marisa, how are you going to live on $7,200 dollars a year?" my mother asked. My father's concerned look mirrored her words.

My childhood was synonymous with the 1950s/60s ideal American middle-class family. If you remember the affable television show *Father Knows Best*, you will get the gist. I was the middle of three children, sandwiched in between my brothers, Christopher and Timothy. We respected, loved, and feared our parents in equal measure. They were definitely in charge. Household rules were strictly enforced and discipline carried out when any of us stepped out of line, which was very rare for me. We were raised to believe, think and behave like our parents and were not really allowed to make decisions on our own. It was out of the question to question them. Deviation from the norm was not an option and neither was compromise in our house—even as my brothers and I grew into young adulthood.

The fact that my parents were questioning my starting salary at WSLS-TV and my ability to be able to live on it worried me. But I knew I had to get my foot in the door of television news, and I knew this was my chance. So, I reassured my parents that I would make it work. It was one of the first adult decisions I made without their guidance or enthusiastic support.

Fortunately for me and my meager budget, a college friend who was already working at the station arranged for me to live with her and two other women, who both worked at other television stations in the Roanoke-Lynchburg market. We lived in an old brick home in the western part of the city that we called "Media West" because of the location and the fact that we all worked in broadcasting. My chunk of the monthly rent? $100.

My father helped me move my belongings to Virginia. A mahogany bed that belonged to my great grandmother, a matching nightstand, bent-wood rocking chair, stereo receiver with a turntable, and a 13-inch black and white TV. I kept that TV for years as a reminder of the humble beginnings of my broadcasting career and where I had to start to "get my foot in the door."

And that first year was tough. After taxes and health insurance, I was taking home far less than $7,200. I could not afford a car, so I bummed rides off my housemates to do errands, go grocery shopping, even to get to work. My dinners mostly consisted of Ramen noodles. Every so often I would splurge on spaghetti sauce and pretend I was having a legitimate pasta dinner. But sometimes I was so hungry that I helped myself to leftovers my housemates kept in the refrigerator. They knew I was taking their food, but never said anything. Although as tough as it was financially, I didn't care. I was getting work experience in television news and that is what mattered to me.

I spent about 18 months in Roanoke living and working with breathtaking natural beauty all around me. (I always said I wish I could have brought the Blue Ridge Mountains back to Pennsylvania with me.) My first position was as a beat reporter covering local government and school board meetings. Even though I aced my journalism classes at Ithaca, once I got out into the real world, I felt like I did not know anything. But I wanted to learn, and I worked hard. I was promoted to weekend anchor and producer, and finally as weeknight co-anchor. It was a fast track that I did not know I was stepping onto, but the experience helped me make my next move.

My brother Tim, who was a college videography intern at WNEP (he also attended Ithaca and majored in broadcasting), was the one who told me the morning and midday co-anchor position at Newswatch 16 was open. He had overheard people saying that Dorothy Lucy was leaving to take a job in New York.

Right after college and before I left for my job in Roanoke, I had contacted Paul Stueber, who was the news director at WNEP at that time, about job opportunities at the station. Paul was a big, burly guy who looked and sounded like Burl Ives. Having worked in major markets like Detroit, Pittsburgh, Indianapolis, and New York City, Paul had a commanding presence. He knew everything about news and news production.

"You need some professional experience first," Paul had written in a letter. "Come back and see me in about a year."

When Tim told me about Dorothy leaving, I took it as a sign to try again. Since I was now anchoring the 6 and 11 p.m. newscasts in Roanoke, I had the experience Paul told me to go find included on my resume tape. I sent the reel to Paul and crossed my fingers. I was called in for an interview, and soon after, was offered the morning co-anchor/field reporter's job. I could not pack my bags fast enough to return home for my dream job.

When I arrived at WNEP in 1984, I quickly realized that how the television station ran on the inside aligned with its public reputation. The news department was built on a foundation of policies, procedures and impeccable standards that cultivated excellent broadcast journalism, even though Wilkes-Barre/Scranton, PA was the 50th largest market in the nation. The ratings success of the station graced the cover of *Broadcasting Magazine* around the time I started. "America's highest rated newscast is in Wilkes-Barre/Scranton, Pennsylvania," the April 1984 cover read followed by:

"Newswatch 16 at 6 with a 35 rating and a 54 share is seen in more homes than news leaders in many markets almost twice its size."

Ratings are measured in two ways: rating points and share points. So, if the 6 p.m. newscast receives a 35 rating and a 54 share, it means out of all television households in the viewing area, 35 percent were tuned into that broadcast and out of all households with a television currently on, 54 percent were tuned into that newscast. Most television stations would kill for those kinds of numbers. And while those numbers slightly declined over the years as cable and satellite became more popular, Newswatch 16 remained a behemoth in the market and still is today.

The broadcast journalism world always carries a certain level of competition. Most reporters dream of sitting in the anchor seat, but there was not a cut-throat, backstabbing culture at WNEP. We were a team working toward a common goal – to put out the best news possible. The station's motto was (and still is) *Proud to Serve*. And we were all proud to serve everyone in northeastern and central Pennsylvania.

Another unique aspect was low turnover. People who were hired at WNEP eventually settled into northeastern Pennsylvania – got married, had children, bought homes, raised their families and became a part of the community. It was easy to get into that comfort zone and decide to stay. I definitely did. Once I returned, I never thought about going after a larger market like Philadelphia again. I felt so fortunate that this was my home. Where you are born and bred and have the chance as a broadcast journalist to work in that area, is just far different from going to another part of the country. You have the competitive edge because you know the area, demographics, streets, roads, terrain, and most importantly the people. You know how long it takes to get from Bloomsburg to Stroudsburg. You just know because you were born in the area. You grew up in the area. That gave me confidence to keep moving toward my goal of becoming lead anchor. I don't think it would have happened if I had been an outsider.

When I started at WNEP, the station was located near the Wilkes-Barre/Scranton International Airport near Avoca. Most of production and administrative offices were in a building, but the newsroom was in two double-wide trailers that were attached to the rest of the property. The WNEP newsroom consisted of big, clunky desks in rows, filthy carpet, and an ever-present curtain of cigarette smoke. Associated Press machines rhythmically printed out the latest breaking news from around the globe while the anchors tapped on electronic typewriters. Reporters had to resort to manual ones. When scripts were finished, the pages were scotch taped together and fed into the teleprompter. Police scanners constantly blared from the assignment desk. Factor in a news producer periodically yelling about whether a story would make deadline, and the newsroom was filled with nerve-racking noise levels. But it was exhilarating and fun.

It seemed to me as though the news department had everything: live trucks that allowed reporters to go live from the scene of breaking news, countless news vehicles to transport crews and equipment, and even a helicopter named Skycam 16. The weather forecasts were done like no other in the nation: from an outdoor set and aptly dubbed, "Weather from the Backyard." Reporters were seasoned journalists and put together dynamite, enterprising stories day after day, night after night. Newswatch 16 was the leader in local and breaking news. By 1985, the 6 p.m. newscast became the highest rated local news broadcast in the country.

WNEP was the premier television station. As much as the Newswatch 16 brand was admired by viewers all over northeastern and central Pennsylvania, WNEP itself was known for broadcasting the big Saint Patrick's parade in Scranton, the Children's Miracle Network telethon, and the Jerry Lewis Muscular Dystrophy telethon every Labor Day along with many other special events. Hatchy Milatchy, a daily children's program with Miss Judy played by Lois Burns, was extremely popular and was still airing when I started at WNEP. It was thrilling to be working at a television station that was so committed to the community. Number one in the market, we left the competition in the dust.

Since I was hired as a morning reporter and co-anchor of the 6:30 a.m. and noon news, my days started by being at work by 5 a.m. I primarily did live reports "out in the field" when I was not inside anchoring the news with Frank Andrews. And I did this for three years.

I never had the opportunity to go live when working in Roanoke. The station just did not have the technological capabilities at that time. So, my first chance to do so was at WNEP. And what a disaster it was…

I was assigned to do an interview with Luzerne County Commissioner Frank Trinisewski. *My God, my first live interview, and he has to have a Polish last name? I will never be able to pronounce his last name correctly,* I thought. What a test, and one that I failed! Not only did I annihilate the commissioner's name, I was so scared about going live that my voice was quivering beyond control. Viewers probably thought I was about to break down in tears!

After it was over, all I could think was *I've ruined my career at WNEP before it barely began*. But when I returned to the station, Paul and I talked about my horrible opening-day performance and what I could have done better, besides pronouncing names the right way. That was the first of many lessons I would learn from him. His guidance, philosophies, standards, values, and news judgment not only helped me hone my broadcast skills, but really shaped Newswatch 16 into the force it still is today.

Like most things in life, the more you practice, the better you get, and I would like to think that I improved with each live shot I did. And honestly, I liked being out in the field more than anything else. But when my co-anchor and producer kept me inside to anchor the noon news, I welcomed that as well because I wanted to get more experience in the anchor chair, too.

I became famous for my reports on road conditions during a snowstorm with the temperature below zero. I also became known for the outfit I wore to try to stay warm: a white snowsuit that made me look like the Michelin Man. On frigid days, when I was not too happy about being out in those severe temps, everything was covered except my eyes. Yes, even my mouth! People tuned into us since we were the only game in town at that time to turn to in the morning for road reports and the latest information that broke overnight. Our ratings at 6:30 a.m. were through the roof.

When you are in the field, you work closely with a photographer. It was a team effort, pure and simple. A water main break. A crash. A fire. We would get in the news vehicle and head out to wherever there was a story. If it happened to be a slow morning, we would tape fronts like "later today here at the courthouse…" We'd go live between 6:30 and 7:00 a.m., and during 7:25 and 8:25 a.m. cut-ins when network tossed to local. Then, a quick phone call to our noon producer Frank Andrews about what taped story we would send in that morning. Live at noon, usually with a full-fledged story, before calling it day at 12:30 p.m.

I was young, enthusiastic and hungry for the experience. I wanted to work. Yes, when the alarm went off at 4:00 a.m., it was tough to get up, but it was my job, and I was grateful for it.

At the end of 1985 WNEP was bought by one of the most respected and prestigious news organizations in the world: *The New York Times*. The company invested millions of dollars in the station making even more improvements in equipment. In 1989 the station moved to a new state-of-the-art studio near Montage Mountain outside Scranton. It was the first property at the base of the mountain, so executives had the right to choose its address: 16 Montage Mountain Road. Pretty cool. It was also cool to brag that our station was owned by *The New York Times*.

However, several years of the early morning schedule started taking its toll. So, by the late 1980's and after many requests to be rotated off the early morning shift, management assigned me to a dayside reporter's position, including covering the esteemed Scranton beat, followed by a promotion to anchor the 5 p.m. newscast. Then, in 1990, the coveted and prestigious 6 and 11 p.m. co-anchor spot suddenly opened up after Karen Harch announced she was leaving. Karen married former WNEP sportscaster Alby Oxenreiter, after Alby had landed a job in Pittsburgh. They had a long-distance marriage from March until June of that year, when she also moved to Pittsburgh. She eventually became a reporter in the Steel City as well.

Like me, Karen was born in northeastern Pennsylvania. She was a consummate professional with impeccable reporting and writing skills. She commanded respect in the newsroom and she certainly deserved it. I looked up to her and aspired to be the kind of professional she was. On Karen's last day, Tim Morrissey, the news director who took over after Paul Stueber became a news director in Baltimore, called me into his office. A calm and reserved (most of the time) news director, he wanted nothing but excellence when it came to journalism and expected it from his employees.

"You're already anchoring the five. You're next in line. You're local. You're from Danville. People like you, so we thought you would be the best fit to sit next to Nolan. We're going to draw up a new contract."

Karen left on a Friday. I was sitting in her anchor chair the following Monday. I was 29, and now a main anchor. A dream and a sought-after position I never thought would come so quickly.

Those first few nights on air with Nolan Johannes were surreal. Just a few days earlier, Karen Harch, a respected news writer and broadcast journalist was still in the seat. And now here I was. I thought, *My God, I have big shoes to fill.* I was excited, but nervous. I wanted to be there, but I was very unsure I would be able to do what Karen did. I knew I was nowhere on the journalistic level that Karen had attained. She was my mentor, and now, here I was, trying to be the lead female co-anchor at WNEP! I was suddenly catapulted from a minor player in the newsroom to a major player. And add sitting next to this legend of Nolan Johannes who was one of the most beloved personalities ever in the market.

I remember my first night walking out on the set and being introduced by Nolan as his new partner. The energy was exhilarating, but the nervousness was nearly uncontrollable. I wanted my hair and makeup to be perfect. I wanted to make sure my outfit was impressionable. I practiced to make sure I read every script perfectly to avoid making a mistake on air. That would have been mortifying—especially sitting next to a legend like Nolan.

He was a wizard at connecting with the audience. Nolan came to Newswatch 16 in 1982 with no former news experience. He was a broadcast personality in Buffalo, New York, mostly doing on-air announcements, when the station hired him. He never claimed to be a journalist, but perhaps that's why he was so successful and endearing at WNEP. When he looked into the camera, he was talking to one person, and that was you. No fancy suits or ties. Completely down-to-earth and humble, yet the epitome of class. A gentleman with gentle ways.

He made viewers feel like family. And he did so in a strong, but calming, dignified voice. He was a master at intonation and pacing. He also gave me little lessons on grammar, life, common sense things. One that stuck with me is "a cake is done, your cupcakes are done, but you complete or finish something." He was a person who led by example. I watched and learned.

We became the most-watched anchor team at WNEP, and two of the most recognizable people in northeastern and central Pennsylvania. People asked for our autographs like we were Hollywood celebrities. I relished the notoriety even more since I was a local gal. Back then, I did not think much about what it was like to be on the other side of a newscast, to be the subject of a news story. Never did I think that years later I would find out.

CHAPTER 2

Nolan retired from WNEP nearly two months after I had my first daughter in January of 1996, which happened two years after I married the proverbial man of my dreams I had met on a blind date arranged by a mutual friend, Kelly Rippon. If her last name sounds familiar it is because her eldest child, Adam Rippon, is a former competitive figure skater and Olympic Bronze Medalist. Kelly's husband also worked as a graphic artist at WNEP at the time.

■ ■ ■

It was August 1992. I had just returned from a trip to Houston, Texas where I covered the Republican National Convention and the nominations of George H.W. Bush and Dan Quayle as president and vice president of the United States. Yes, this was still during the days when local affiliates sent their own reporters and anchors to cover national political events. And yes, Houston in August is soupy and sweltering, which did not make my 14-hour workdays while I was there easy. I was physically tired from the heat and mentally tired from the long hours spent with the local northeastern Pennsylvania delegates and generating two or three stories each day.

I returned home exhausted and craving time on the couch with a good movie and air conditioning. But Kelly called. "Marisa, there is someone from high school I want you to meet. I think you might like him," she said. "He's a really good guy from a nice family."

I usually stayed far away from blind dates. I protested a bit. I tried to play the I'm-exhausted-and-need-time-on-the-couch-in-AC card. Kelly kept at it and finally persuaded me with the promise of good food and good company on a laid-back Saturday evening. So, I abandoned my hopes for couch time and headed to Kelly's house in Clarks Summit. And I was so glad I did…

Mark Kandel was the first person I saw when I walked into Kelly's home that night. He looked like an L.L. Bean model dressed in a button-down shirt, khaki shorts and Docksiders. All six foot two of him. He reminded me of Superman's human persona, Clark Kent, with his full head of dark brown hair and amber-beer eyes, minus the eyeglasses.

He introduced himself and joked that he knew what I looked like by "turning on the news." I never met a man more charming and with such a keen sense of humor and split-second wit. His impersonations resembled comedic talents from the likes of Dana Carvey, Martin Short, and Bill Hader-- all wrapped up in one.

Kelly and her husband stepped out of the living room for a while after dinner so Mark and I could talk alone. We shared our likes, our dislikes, hobbies, interests, and backgrounds. In no time, we discovered we had a lot in common (both liked movies, shopping, traveling). After graduating from Scranton Central High School in 1978, Mark went to East Stroudsburg University in Pennsylvania and majored in Special Education, then received his master's degree from Shippensburg University also in PA. The summer I met Mark he was in the midst of completing his Ph.D. in learning disabilities, special education policy and school administration from the University of Maryland and was living off a fellowship. He occasionally drove back to Scranton on the weekends to see his family.

I remember saying to myself that evening, "Well, this will be a delightful experience, but why in the world would a guy like this be interested in someone like me?" My self-doubt always came into play when it came to relationships with guys. My first impression of Mark was that he was in another league, one that I did not have the stats to join. I was short. I was physically fit, but not really athletic. He was tall, athletic, and charming. I could tell that people just gravitated toward him. He was a Ken doll who needed a Barbie, and I was the opposite of her. I never thought I would see or hear from him again. But as we walked to our cars that night at Kelly's house, Mark asked me for my telephone number. I was thrilled! He jotted down my phone number on a piece of paper, escorted me to my car, kissed me on the cheek and said, "I will definitely call you. I want to see you again." I got into my car, and he closed the door like a perfect gentleman. We both left Kelly's at the same time. I remember feeling like I was on cloud nine.

Our first date was a picnic at Lake Winola where Mark's parents were members of the Canoe Club. Mark made an impression by bringing along a picnic basket, filled with grapes, cheese and red wine. We picked a spot and sat down. All of a sudden we noticed bees buzzing around us. It did not take us long to figure out we had sat near a ground nest full of yellow jackets! We quickly moved and then settled into our picnic. We talked for hours as we sat next to the lake in the warmth of the late afternoon August sun.

That night, we went to the movies to see *Single White Female*. Not sure why we chose that. It doesn't seem like the best first-date movie, but we did. I insisted on paying for the tickets. Now, I was doing the impressing. Mark said I did not have to, but I insisted. He thanked me and said it was thoughtful and generous.

After that first date, he headed back to College Park, Maryland for the start of a new semester. And we started a two-year, long-distance relationship. Every two weeks, I would jump in my car as soon as my shift ended and head south on Interstate 81. On the opposite weeks, Mark came back home. It was hard, but we knew it was temporary, so we made it work.

At this time, I was living alone in an apartment in West Pittston. My trips to Maryland were a bit more interesting. Since money was tight for Mark, he took on the responsibility of resident advisor for a fraternity on campus. It meant free room and board while he completed his doctoral coursework, which certainly helped ease the strain on his budget. But our times together while I was visiting, including the private, intimate moments, were usually interrupted by loud, obnoxious frat brothers who loved to party and play loud, obnoxious music well into the middle of the night.

I quickly saw that Mark was like a father to these young men and provided guidance, advice and encouragement whenever needed. So, I did my best to go with the flow in terms of his living arrangements. Again, it was only until he finished graduate school. He enjoyed mentoring them and definitely acted like the adult in charge, but he also joked around with them like a big brother would. He allowed himself to be "one of the boys."

Before the University of Maryland, Mark worked for the Department of Defense as a high-school teacher for students whose parents were stationed at Bitburg Air Force Base in Germany. He took advantage of his five years there to travel all over Europe. He kept his souvenirs from those trips and proudly displayed them in his frat house where they were always conversation starters. Mark was always ready with a story of his travels and his trinkets.

Perhaps it was Mark's travel experiences and his appreciation for diversity that kept him so positive all the time. You never heard him criticize anybody or anything, as he always found the best in people. Connecting with others seemed so natural for him. The world was not always about him. He listened when others spoke, and I think this attracted people to him the way a lamppost harkens moths on a dark summer night.

And then there was that spontaneous sense of humor. He had a knack for doing impersonations that would make everyone laugh until our stomachs ached. I think the fact that he made me laugh every single day was one of the things I found most attractive about him. No other man I had ever dated made me laugh like that. But I also loved that he was a gentleman who opened doors; a romantic who wrote thoughtful messages in every card he gave me; a man who sent flowers on birthdays and Valentine's Day. He made me feel important. His life revolved around me and mine around his. I just felt so safe and secure in our relationship. I fell in love with him, and I fell hard.

In March 1993, just seven months after Mark and I met, we decided to head south for spring break on our first vacation together. Mark's parents owned a condominium in Bradenton, a Florida gulf-coast retirement community between Sarasota and Tampa, where they spent winters. We would get to spend time with them as well and relax on the beach with a Gulf view.

The plan was for me to drive to Maryland and then Mark and I would fly to Florida from Washington D.C. Before I left, Mark's younger sister Kim, who lived in Scranton, dropped off a sealed box and asked me to take it to her brother. She innocently described it as a care package.

"He knows it's coming," she said without giving me any more details about the contents.

Mark and I were so excited about our trip, but when I arrived in Maryland, he seemed a bit nervous. He asked me for the box, I took it out of my bag and handed it over. He never opened it in front of me, and I did not ask any questions. We flew out the next morning.

That week, cool temperatures blanketed Florida and gusty winds blew. It was the backside of the blizzard of '93 that was marching its way through the northeast. But Mark still insisted we venture to the beach. His mom knew what was about to happen. She had tears in her eyes as we headed out. I did not stop to think about the why behind the tears.

We huddled together on a blanket with another one wrapped around us. The often-calm Gulf was kicking up some waves. Sand blew around. Not my ideal beach day, but at least I was getting to spend time with Mark. Suddenly and seemingly out of nowhere, he pulled out a stuffed animal of two dinosaurs embracing.

"Folklore has it that when two dinosaurs found true love," he said, "they would seal their bond like this." At that moment, he turned around the stuffed animal, and on one of the dinosaur tails was a diamond ring.

Even before he could get the words out, we both began to cry.

After a few minutes he was able to manage, "Will you marry me?"

"Yes!" I said enthusiastically as I held out my hand for him to put the ring on.

I suddenly also realized what was in that box. Mark had ordered the diamond ring and had it sized to fit my finger at a jewelry store back home in Danville. Rather than send the ring through the mail, Mark and his sister concocted a plan to have me transport my own engagement ring. So, unbeknownst to me, I traveled from Pennsylvania to Maryland with my own ring in tow.

We set July 16, 1994 as our wedding date to give us time to plan. I had always wanted a big, formal wedding with all the lavish fairy-tale details and that is what we had in my hometown of Danville at The Basilica of Saints Cyril and Methodius. It was, and still is, used as the convent chapel for the nuns at their mother house, Villa Sacred Heart. The distinguished bell tower is a landmark in Danville. But inside, marble, mosaics and stained glass fill this majestic chapel. I felt like Maria from *The Sound of Music* walking down the long aisle. I didn't see our family and friends in the pews. My eyes were on Mark waiting for me at the altar. At the same time, WNEP sent a news crew to our wedding ceremony and a good portion of the video that was shot aired that night during the weekend news. When a significant life event occurred with our on-air people, the station made it a point to cover it because it made the viewers immediately become part of "our" family.

After a traditional Roman Catholic wedding ceremony, the fairy tale continued at our reception on the campus of Bucknell University with nearly 200 guests where we ate, danced, and laughed well into the night. A night I never wanted to end.

Mark had reserved a suite at the Inn at Turkey Hill not far from Danville for our wedding night. We arrived late after our long, memorable day, but he had already arranged to have flowers and candles for our romantic night. He carried me over the threshold, and a few minutes later started a bubble bath in the jacuzzi for us to enjoy as a married couple. And then it hit me. I stood there frozen in front of him. I suddenly realized my name legally changed from Burke to Kandel. That I was going to share the rest of my life with this man. And all the excitement of preparing for our wedding was over in an instant. That huge letdown and the realization that I was now married with a new last name overwhelmed me. I started crying uncontrollably. Mark, who wanted the night to be perfect for me, could have easily snapped in disgust and disappointment. But he did not. He sat on the edge of the bed holding me close and repeating, "It's okay honey. Let it out. This is a huge change for you." Because of my mood, we never had sex on our wedding night.

A few days later, we left for our honeymoon, which I thought was going to be spent at his parents' Florida condo, empty during the summer when his folks were back in Scranton. But Mark surprised me and instead of flying to Tampa, we flew to Miami for a cruise to the Bahamas. On that trip, we just could not get enough of each other. We were riding the wave of honeymoon bliss. Every day was filled with tropical fun, gourmet food and of course, laughter. Lots of laughter. And I felt like the luckiest woman on the planet; my head filled with beautiful memories of a story-book wedding and married to a man who truly cared about making me happy. And finally, the fulfillment I longed for in my personal life to balance the success of my professional life! My life felt so complete.

CHAPTER 3

Mark grew up in Green Ridge, a Scranton neighborhood filled with big, older homes and tree-lined streets. Green Ridge was, and still is, known as one of the finest residential sections of Scranton. Many of the city's most prominent citizens—mayors, bankers, doctors, and attorneys – call it home. And now that we were married, it seemed like the logical next step to look for a house there.

At the time, we were living in an apartment in another part of Scranton and Mark was still working on his doctorate. We were managing on just my salary, but we were not going for extravagant during our house hunt. The first time I stepped through the front door of a two-story colonial on Richmont Street, built in 1925, I knew it was just right for us.

When we bought the house for just $94,000, we thought we were getting a steal. Unfortunately, the sellers were going through a divorce. But they were in a hurry to sell, so their misfortune actually played to our benefit. Our first home had four bedrooms, two full baths, a grand front porch, a gorgeous eat-in kitchen with cherry cabinets, and a manicured backyard. The day after we moved in, we started renovations to update both bathrooms and to finish the third floor, which Mark made into his office.

Wedding: check.

First home: check.

And as the saying goes, "new house, new baby." Two months after moving, I found out I was pregnant.

Not long after, Mark turned to me and asked, "How would you feel if I ran for Scranton School Board?"

My first reaction was surprise. I was counting on Mark's undivided attention during my pregnancy. I also knew that because of my job in television news, it would be ethically impossible for me to campaign with him. After just buying a house, being in the midst of renovations, and preparing for the arrival of a baby, I was concerned about the financial investment of a campaign. But Mark was fascinated by politics and was a strong advocate for public education. He and his siblings were educated in public schools. So, he thought running for school board was a logical next step. He was especially excited to hear about the plans to build a new high school in Scranton and knew that by serving as a school board director, he could have a direct impact on how those plans would be carried out. I understood all of that.

"If this is what's in your heart, then go for it," I said. "Just keep in mind that we can't even think about putting a political sign in our own front yard because of my job. And obviously, I can't campaign with you."

Personally, I never understood why anyone would want the hassle of being a school board director. It's a thankless job, without pay, and you're scrutinized for everything you say or do. It's the epitome of the adage, "*You can't please all of the people all of the time.*" I knew this because my father served on the school board in the Danville Area School District in the 1970s. He would often say how he had to make sure to choose every word on record carefully to avoid anything he said being misconstrued.

But that didn't matter to Mark. He was ready for the challenge of being the only republican candidate in a city where democrats outnumber republicans two to one. Mark knew what a challenge it would be, but he spent nights and weekends going door to door, passing out fliers and talking with voters. Whenever we went out, whether it was to church or to the supermarket, he campaigned and did it well. He truly stood out from the other candidates. He was well-educated and could talk about everything and anything – from politics to sports. He knew how to connect with people; knew when to turn on his sense of humor and turn up his charm. And he always knew just the right thing to say with perfect nuance and rhythm.

A conversation with the older ladies would always end with a compliment like, "What a nice scarf that is you're wearing," or "That hairstyle really becomes you." The women melted from his attention.

Mark was in his element.

But what may have helped Mark's chances of winning more than anything else was the fact that he had a celebrity wife. While he could not publicize any image of himself with me or promote his cause using my status, we were out in public enough together for people to know we were husband and wife. Mark also admitted to me, not so much out of guilt but with amusement, that when he went door-to-door to campaign, conversations would inevitably evolve into, "You may know my wife, Marisa Burke? She's the anchorwoman on WNEP-16." By dropping that line, Mark told me that people were much more receptive to what he had to say and paid more attention.

Whether that made a difference or not remains unknown, but Mark easily won a school-board seat in Scranton that November. The local newspaper ran a huge article about his victory since a republican won in a city dominated by democrats. He was so proud of his victory. So was I.

By December, I was nine months pregnant and felt like the size of a house. But I stood, holding the bible, between the judge and my husband as he took his oath of office. Spectators to the swearing-in ceremony were all around us, snapping photos. I felt like it was the paparazzi. Mark soaked up the adulation. Within a matter of moments, Mark was one of the newest Scranton School Board Directors. I barely got to give him a congratulatory kiss when he was tugged away by other board members, school administrators and news photographers in attendance.

Mark's new position suddenly thrust us into new social circles. In the past, my job had kept us busy with fundraisers, galas, and civic events tied to station sponsorships, but nothing like the events that now began to quickly fill our calendar because of Mark's election to the school board. I realized that 1996 was going to be a very busy year for us.

When you hold public office, everyone suddenly becomes your friend. Mark and I received so many poinsettias and baskets that Christmas season after the election, we gave many of them to family and friends. That Christmas we were also invited to the school superintendent's annual holiday party at his home. In attendance were various city and county leaders, prominent attorneys, along with the who's who of Scranton. This was Mark's first big opportunity to showcase his incredible sense of humor. He did so by doing impersonations of some 'notables' associated with the Scranton School District who didn't have the greatest reputations, and therefore, were absent from the holiday party. Within minutes, Mark had everybody laughing hysterically. I kept thinking to myself, *I am so lucky to be married to this man who so easily can entertain others.*

Mark certainly enjoyed the notoriety and attention. But his biggest sense of accomplishment from his time on the school board was helping approve and oversee the construction of the new Scranton High School. He treasured the shovel he used to turn over the dirt and beamed when his name was engraved on a plaque that hangs in the school. After all, he had attended Scranton schools as did his father. It meant the world to Mark to help shape the future of the Scranton School District and to provide a better learning environment for its students.

■　　■　　■

January 5, 1996. It was love at first sight for Mark and me when Rachael Marie Kandel entered the world. Because she was breach a month before her due date, my doctor and his team kneaded my big belly as if it was bread dough to get her to flip. It didn't work. So, in for a scheduled C-section I went. Mark donned hospital gear and stayed by my side where he could watch the birth. As they pulled her out, I glanced over at Mark and he had tears in his eyes. As much as Mark wanted a son to be his first-born, he was thrilled with his beautiful, healthy daughter. He was ready to be a dad.

Mark looked at me, caressed my hair, held my hand, and whispered, "We have a daughter, and she's beautiful like her mom."

We chose the name Rachael after my maternal grandmother and because Mark wanted a biblical name.

After I got settled in my hospital room, Mark called WNEP to share our good news. He had barely hung up the phone when I looked up at the television to see Rachael's birth announcement crawling across the bottom of the screen like it was "breaking" news. This delighted Mark and hospital staff, but I thought it was way overdone and exaggerated. Even so, I knew that viewers would want to know. Throughout my pregnancy, I received hundreds of baby gifts - beautiful crocheted booties, afghans, baby sweaters. Because of the volume, I had no choice but to donate many of the gifts to charity shops.

As the anesthesia wore off from the cesarean operation, the pain skyrocketed. I was definitely uncomfortable. But just a few hours after Rachael's birth, there was a WNEP camera in my room. I had a feeling the station would want pictures for the news, but I was surprised by how quickly the photographer arrived.

In the true anchorwoman spirit, I applied eye shadow and mascara. I was not allowed to sit up, so I was lying down holding Rachael. Mark sat next to my bed. The news of her arrival was featured on the evening news and well wishes poured into the station.

But the cameras were not always in my room as I continued to recuperate. And neither was Mark. And it was during one of those times when I was alone that I opened my eyes to see a strange, middle-aged man standing at the foot of my bed.

"Hello, Marisa Burke," he said. "I just wanted to come and congratulate you on having a baby."

I was startled and scared but did not feel threatened. I was wondering how he was able just waltz right into my room! Within a minute, hospital personnel came running and escorted him out. The encounter left me shaken and feeling vulnerable. No one seemed to have an answer as to how he had gotten past security, and of course, hospital administrators profusely apologized. I now could relate to Hollywood celebrities who feel violated when crazed fans enter their personal space!

That was not the end of the excitement. The day after Rachael was born, the blizzard of '96 arrived bringing three feet of snow between January 6 and 8. The governor banned most travel, so Mark, Rachael and I were stuck at the hospital for several days longer than expected.

While we were still reveling in the joy of being new parents at home, Mark and I were also sleep-deprived and struggling to adjust. Rachael was a happy baby, but because she had been breach, her hips were dislocated, and she was not sleeping well. A month after her birth, I was a new mommy whose hormones were still all over the place and who was not happy with how slowly my baby belly was disappearing. But Nolan Johannes was retiring due to health reasons,

Hello,

Marissa needs to go get checked for HIV and other diseases sexually transmitted. Her husband, pecmanfrompa, or Matt, as he is known as in the gay community has been sleeping with anything 18 and under from before I think they were married.

After hearing she caught him in bed with a 16 year old boy the room scrantonpam4m on aol has been buzzing about who was with him and who was not and let me tell you the sloth was with more people than could be counted and there were people in the mess he was poking that were infected because names were being named last night by horrible hamlet at aol.

Also, if he deleted his screenname, on aol, you can go in and undelete it and go in the room Scrantonpam4m to confirm his sloths antics. I feel HORRIBLE for Marissa as she is such a wonderful woman to have this fall on her head with two beautiful girls. I would never let that scumbag see them again.

Oh and wanna talk about the boys in the locker room he molested at the U of S. and was turned into perverted justice and they will post his name and all chat logs. He would never send his pic so they were sending a decoy to meet him and hopefully she caught this just in time.

I hope all her co-workers will rally around her and hold her up during what may be trying times for her..as I said she is to BEAUTIFUL and caring person to have this happen to her. I know what a caring person she is and Joe, you're a good dude, take care of her please. We all love her in this room and no one ever knew pecman was her husband until recently or people would have told her and stayed away from him but he has been slothing for boys before they were even married or had the girls.

Please, Please help her through this emotionally…you're a family…and take him to the cleaners people.

And then:

ScrantonpaM4m RoomDear Webmaster:

Please tell Marissa her husband (pecmanfrompa) has been fooling around with boys in the scrantonpam4m aol room for the past 8 years at least. He had boys over last week. This is not new to him. I could tell her stories that will make her hair curl and I feel so so bad about what he did but I just found out who he was.

There are a lot of people in this room that will attest to he what he has been doing, but the only thing I would have her do is get tested for hiv. That is first and foremost. Then clean his clock cause he is nothing but scum and everyone knows it in here and that is all the talk that is going around. If you need further information as to what he was doing don't you or marissa hesitate to contact this email address. I saw her have those little babies. I remember when she married the child molester. What a sad day this has become.

I suspected that the emails were written by the same person because of their similarities, but they originated from different addresses. One was hidden; the other came from "Thickhardd1ck."

Filthy and disgusting were the only two words that came to mind. As embarrassed as I was, my defenses also went up big-time. This idiot or idiots were trying to say that my husband took part in lewd chatrooms designated for homosexuals and child molesters. *Nothing could be further from the truth,* I thought. And if they were so intent on letting the world know about what they thought they knew about Mark—why didn't they put their real name out there instead of hiding behind some moniker? Newsroom personnel receive hundreds of emails a day. Many are legitimate and signed by the sender. But many others are sent by people just looking to be seen and heard, even when they do not sign their real names. I vowed not to get upset about such trash and wanted to dismiss it as another case of some cruel viewer trying to embarrass a person with celebrity status just to make themselves feel better.

But, these two emails disturbed me unlike any other emails I had received through the years. As much as I wanted to know why these emails were sent and why they said what they did, I chose not to discuss them with Mark. Instead, I chose to put them in the back of my mind so as not to embarrass him.

In the end, this temporary assignment became permanent. I was still producing and anchoring the 6 p.m. news when I left WNEP in 2016.

■　■　■

I guess the next step in home ownership is often renovations. Since we bought our house new, the only living space that wasn't complete was the basement. I thought the main living floors were enough for our family, so I was in no rush to finish the basement. But Mark painted a picture of renovating the basement as being a place where we could hang out as a family, and later as the girls got older, they could use it as a gathering space for friends. He won me over.

We worked together on the design to include an exercise room, TV room, full bath, game room and a bar, complete with a beer tap coming out of the wall. The renovation project took more than a year to complete. But when the basement was finished, furnished, and decorated, the area had turned into a haven for future holiday gatherings, super bowl parties, and movie-watching with the girls. It was the perfect spot to let loose and have fun.

An avid sports fan who could spit out stats and recite trivia with ease, Mark decorated the game room with all sorts of sports memorabilia that was authentic and expensive. Whether it was a football autographed by famed Green Bay quarterback Brett Favre or a jersey signed by NHL star Sidney Crosby, it started appearing in our basement. And I wondered how Mark was paying for all of it.

"Hey honey, I love the sports items you are hanging up in the basement and everything looks great," I said. "But how much is this stuff costing?"

I didn't bring up money often. I had my own checking account and credit cards, and Mark had his. I paid the household utilities. He paid for the vacations. Now that Mark had a decent-paying job, we split the cost of the monthly mortgage. He assumed responsibility for paying the monthly payments on the $100,000 home equity loan we took out to renovate the basement.

I always thought personal finances like separate checking accounts, should be kept private, even between a husband and wife. We never outright discussed this before or during our marriage. It was just something we both assumed and were comfortable with. Our opinions organically meshed on this. We never argued about money. But I felt as if I had to ask about what I thought was extravagant spending.

"I bid on eBay for the sports things," Mark said. "I thought they would look nice in the game room, and they will only increase in value."

Our exercise room was a dream for this busy, working mom. It had a tread mill, elliptical machine, strength-training equipment and a full set of dumbbells. A full-length mirror hung on one wall with a television above it to make the time on the treadmill go by more quickly. I loved having a mini-gym at home, so I did not have to spend time running back and forth to a commercial one. Mark was adamant about including this room in our renovation plans. I thought the time-saving convenience would work just as well for him as it did for me. So I never understood why Mark still maintained a gym membership, but he did. And usually after dinner, he headed for the gym and would be gone for several hours.

Again, I questioned him about the money he was spending. "I don't get why you are going to a gym when we have all that gym equipment downstairs," I asked him. "You spent all this money on everything in the basement. Why the need to go to a gym?"

"Because the gym has much more equipment that I can use; stuff we don't have here." Mark explained. "And besides, I have a lot of friends at the gym."

I knew this to be true because he would come home and talk about the conversations he had with various guys. One of them was a body builder. Even though he was a man half the age of Mark, they started hanging out together. I met him when he stopped by the house to see Mark, and he was gorgeous. He had the physique of Dwayne "The Rock" Johnson as well as Hollywood looks—striking blond hair and piercing blue eyes. Mark said his bodybuilder friend taught him fitness and nutrition techniques.

Perhaps Mark's acquaintances at the gym were letting others know about his availability to tutor because more and more young guys were showing up at the house for help. I would be working in the kitchen or playing with the girls, when I would hear the doorbell ring. Mark always answered the front door. If I happened to look his way from down the long, center hallway, he would introduce the student by name and say something like, "He came over so I could help him write and edit his research paper." It never seemed like these students showed up unannounced. It appeared as though Mark was always expecting them. After the brief introductions, Mark would lead them into his office in the front of the house; quite a distance from the kitchen. He shut the door for privacy, and I rarely heard the conversations.

Mark never turned away any of the young men even when they showed up late in the evening. Despite the obvious generation gap, he insisted that he was just a "mentor" and "teacher" to these young men. "Nothing more," he insisted. I trusted him. Why wouldn't I?

CHAPTER 5

Spring 2008. The days were getting longer, the air warmer. The trees had new leaves and flowers were blooming everywhere. Everything felt new and fresh. Rachael and Sarah were weeks away from finishing sixth and fifth grades. They were looking forward to summer break, sleeping in, swimming in the pool, and spending time with friends.

But, for now, they were looking forward to a weekend trip to visit my mom in the Danville area. She was a nana who loved to spoil her granddaughters. The girls knew that a trip to her house in the spring and summer also meant a trip to one of their favorite places, Knoebels Amusement Resort; a family-owned amusement park that's been around since the 1920's, and only twenty minutes from our homestead in Riverside, the small borough right across the Susquehanna River from Danville.

On Friday, I rushed home from work to pack up and head out with the girls so we could spend the weekend celebrating Mother's Day and my mom's 79th birthday. Mark was never a big fan of going to my mother's house, so it did not surprise me when he decided to stay home. But he also insisted that he would spend the weekend doing spring clean-up and getting the pool in shape, which needed attention after another long winter. He encouraged me to take the girls and promised we would celebrate Mother's Day as a family when we returned on Sunday.

The girls, my mom and I had a great time at Knoebels. My mom had fun watching the girls jump from ride to ride. On Mother's Day we got up early and went to mass. It gave my mother joy showing off her granddaughters to her church friends. She also loved going out with me whenever I went home since I was a regional celebrity. When people fawned all over me, they paid attention to my mother, and she relished that adulation.

Mark had dinner waiting for us when the girls and I returned to Peckville that evening, and several Mother's Day gifts were sitting, neatly wrapped, on the kitchen table. He had a big smile on his face as the girls recounted their visit to Knoebels and to nana's house. He was totally engaged in their conversation being the attentive daddy he always was.

A few weeks later, I was at work when my cell phone rang. It was Mark and what he had to say suddenly turned my life upside down.

"Honey?" he said, "I am at the District Attorney's office. It appears I might be in some trouble because of a party at the house."

"Party? What party?" I asked nervously. "And when?"

"I had a gathering at the house the weekend you and the girls were away. Just some guys I knew from the gym," he responded.

"What guys? How many? How old were they?" I snapped back. I had a hundred more questions racing through my mind. I couldn't ask them fast enough.

"They are all in college," he answered, "except for one who is still in high school, and I think it's because of him that I'm in trouble."

At this point, Mark's answers were becoming a blur. "What happens now?" I asked.

Mark responded, "I think if I cooperate with the authorities everything will be okay. They just want me to sign some papers."

"Sign papers!" I exclaimed, "Don't you think you should contact an attorney first?"

Instead of answering, Mark quickly ended the conversation. "I have to go, honey. We'll talk more when you get home," he said.

Mark seemed too calm and collected for this to be any more than a misunderstanding or misrepresentation, I thought. I hung up the phone and tried to stay focused on news for the rest of the afternoon. It wasn't long after Mark's phone call that I received another one. This time the call came from the Lackawanna County Assistant District Attorney, Gene Talerico.

Talerico became the first assistant district attorney in 2000 when his boss Andy Jarbola was appointed district attorney. He was a formidable force in the courtroom and relentless when it came to prosecuting child victim cases in Lackawanna County. We knew each other professionally. I had interviewed him several times regarding criminal cases that made the news, but nothing could have prepared me for what I was about to hear from him now.

"Marisa," he said, "you know your husband is in serious trouble. We are looking at charging him with a number of crimes, including corruption of minors."

The fear and anxiety hit me like a rogue wave. I felt like throwing up. Mark made it sound as if what happened was a minor infraction. And now I have the assistant DA on the phone telling me, in so many words, that Mark could be facing jail time! The anguish I felt left me absolutely numb. I knew I had to get home and talk with Mark face-to-face to learn the facts about what happened that weekend the girls and I were away at my mom's house.

When I arrived home, Mark appeared surprisingly composed. He refused to give me names of the guys who attended the party, implying that I did not know them anyway. They were just people he knew through his connections to the colleges and universities in the area, the guys he tutored, and through friends he made at the gym. Mark continued to downplay what happened.

"It was just a bunch of guys getting together," he insisted. "I think the trouble-maker is a 17-year-old boy who snuck in, stole some beer, left, was out all night with his buddies, and when his mother caught him, he said he was drinking here and blamed everything on me. He wasn't even invited. He came here on his own because he knew some others who were here."

Even though I felt very uneasy about Mark's cryptic explanation, I accepted it, because I believed him. It sounded as though this teenager was making Mark the "fall guy" after the trouble he got into with his mother. Yet, my stomach was still churning as I processed it all.

How would we tell the girls? How much will be made public? How would Mark's boss at NEIU 19 react? What will WNEP say? And how serious are the charges going to be?

In the days that followed I tried my best to pretend that everything was normal, both at work and at home in front of the girls, but my insides were in knots. I was scared about what could come next. There was actually a small ounce of relief when we heard that the District Attorney's office had filed its criminal complaint at a magistrate's office in Peckville. One count of selling or furnishing alcohol to minors, a misdemeanor in the third degree, was a crime far less severe than corrupting the morals of a minor. The charge would be sent through the mail, also somewhat of a relief to me, because charges or citations sent through the mail usually mean they are less severe, and therefore, do not attract that much attention.

But as a journalist, I knew that prosecutors are motivated by high-profile cases that involve high-profile people. And even though Mark's case involved a "minor" charge, we were talking about an educator with a doctorate degree, a former Scranton school director, a member of several educational advisory boards, and the husband of Marisa Burke.

On the day the charge was filed against Mark, we were getting ready to leave for Michigan to attend my niece's high-school graduation in Ann Arbor. Before I left, I thought it best to give my bosses a heads-up about the charge.

"Mark made a mistake," I said. "He regrets it, and I believe that's all there's to it."

If only it had been that simple.

■　　■　　■

During the eight-hour ride to Michigan, Mark and I did not talk much, but we both tried to act as normal as possible for the sake of the girls who still didn't know the predicament their father was in. I watched the mile markers slip by. We left Pennsylvania, passed through Ohio, and drew closer to the Michigan state line, and the what ifs piled up in my mind like a traffic jam.

That evening, after we arrived at my brother's house, my cell phone rang. I recognized the number. I had a feeling it would be either my current news director, Eric Schrader or perhaps even the general manager, Lou Kirchen. Both ended up being on the phone.

"Marisa, it's Eric. Lou Kirchen is also in the room, and we have you on speaker phone. Channel 28 (the NBC affiliate in the Wilkes-Barre/Scranton market) made a pretty big deal out of what you told me about Mark. I was under the impression from you that this was going to be a minor infraction against him. But because he is an educator and on education advisory boards, we have to report something because he is accused of furnishing alcohol to minors," Eric explained.

They had just watched our competition going "live" at 6 and what added insult to injury was that Mark's case was their lead story! They described in detail what the story said and looked like on air, including shots of our house in Peckville and their reporter knocking on the door of our home, seeking comment from Mark.

When they mentioned that, I trembled. *My home on TV*. Showing reporters knocking on the doors of someone accused of wrongdoing is typical in television news. *But this was my house! How dare they do something so awful!* The horror I felt being on the opposite side of a news story. And of course, the Channel 28 reporter tagged out his story by saying, "Mark Kandel is the husband of WNEP-TV anchorwoman, Marisa Burke."

As much as I thought it was a low blow from the competition, I was still mortified. *They did this on purpose to make me and WNEP look bad,* I kept saying to myself in anger.

My bosses were disappointed and concerned. Until they watched what was being reported on the other stations, our news department was not even going to do a story. But now they had no choice.

WNEP quickly changed course. Station management did not want to appear that we were ignoring the story to favor me. So, by the 7 o'clock news that evening, WNEP began airing Mark's story. The following script aired during that newscast:

"A former Scranton School Board member is charged with providing alcohol to minors. The Lackawanna District Attorney's office says Mark Kandel gave beer and liquor to a dozen minors at a party at his house. Kandel is on the board of directors for the Pennsylvania Council for Exceptional Children. If convicted of the misdemeanor, he could face a year in the Lackawanna County jail, or a 25-hundred dollar fine."

But unlike the competition, the initial story Newswatch 16 aired made no mention that I was the wife of Mark Kandel.

Even so, I thought, *my God, how could this be happening?* Our lives were so perfect. Mark was well-respected as an educator. I was one of the most recognized personalities in the area. We had two amazing daughters, a beautiful home, and wonderful family and friends.

Why was Mark's minor charge being blown up to be such a major story? Then it hit me. Big names attract a lot of attention. To me, it appeared that the DA's office tipped off the competition as well as the newspapers because of who was involved and Mark was married to me. Scandal involving people of local celebrity status. I was the big trophy that the DA's office could show off on its mantel. How could I be so gullible and naïve to think Mark's case would not become a major local news story?

The following day was perhaps even worse for WNEP. Viewers certainly learned what was broadcast on the other stations, and WNEP was under fire. It appeared to our viewers that not only was the station trying to downplay the story but was also trying to protect its main anchor by not mentioning Mark's connection to me in the news reports.

Station management never contacted me again while I was in Michigan. Perhaps they did not want my time away ruined more than it was. Perhaps it was because it was almost the weekend. But right before that, WNEP tried to redeem itself using a platform called Talkback 16, which allows viewers to call in, make suggestions, complain, or in rare cases, pass along a compliment. The calls are recorded on a special line, and a producer chooses which comments should be aired. The Talkback 16 calls are played at the end of the 5:30 newscast and right before the 6 p.m. The comment section has been one of Newswatch 16's most popular segments since its inception in 1993. Anyone and anything are fair game.

Sometimes viewers' suggestions or opinions are taken seriously by station management. Up until now, viewers may have commented on my hair, or my clothes, but nothing like what was directed at me now. The following is what aired the day after the news broke about Mark:

Anchor: "A former Scranton School Board member is accused of giving alcohol to minors. In tonight's Talkback 16, callers accuse the News Station of trying to cover up the story because of the man's connections to one of our employees."

Caller: "Your 15 second blurb about Marisa's husband was disgusting at 11 o'clock tonight. What the hell's the matter with you people? You say you're the number one news station. You're repulsive. Just because she's one of your own, you're going to protect her? That's bull(bleep) and you people know better."

Caller: "The 7 o'clock news and 11 o'clock news today on Thursday had the station reporting that Mr. Kandel has been arrested for furnishing alcohol to minors at his home. Last I knew his home was Marisa Burke's home. How come you didn't mention that? I'm sure this will never make air."

Caller: "Yes, I'd like to know why you're not shoving the camera in Marisa Burke's face and knock on her door asking about the underage drinking party with children at her house. How come you aren't shoving the camera in her face? You do it to everybody else. What's the matter? You don't like it now that the story is on your side that's no good?"

The anchor then read this on camera:

"Newswatch 16 did report the story about the misdemeanor charges against Mark Kandel on Newswatch 16 at 7, 11 and again several times on Newswatch 16 This Morning. The story has also been posted on wnep.com since last evening. Mark Kandel is not an employee of WNEP-TV. Marisa Burke, our employee, was not named in the charges and is therefore not part of the story."

I was somewhat relieved to hear that WNEP had issued this kind of response. The station's approach to all those negative comments showed that management trusted what I had originally told them and certainly gave me the benefit of the doubt, even though many viewers thought I was receiving special treatment. For the first time, though, I was on the receiving end of severe and painful Talkback 16 criticism, and it hurt. The calls were broadcast all over northeastern and central Pennsylvania. So, not only strangers, but family, friends, people in my hometown heard the nasty comments. I was the main anchor, the person people looked up to, the respected one in the community, and now I felt like trash. Did our viewers really feel this way toward me? Viewers also didn't know that while all this was breaking, I was still in Michigan, so my absence on the air raised even more suspicion.

We were in Michigan to celebrate my niece's high-school graduation, and I decided to focus on that. I refused to cast a shadow over her accomplishment. I did not say a word to the rest of the family about what was going on at home until right before we were leaving my older brother's home. Then I asked both him and my younger brother who was also there for the graduation, if we could talk in private. The three of us left the rest of the family on the first floor while we went downstairs to my brother's basement. They sat on the couch, and I sat in a chair facing them.

"There's something I need to tell the both of you before we head back to Pennsylvania," I said anxiously.

My two brothers looked at each other, and their faces turned pale.

I proceeded, "Mark has gotten himself into trouble with the law. He had a party where some college-age students were drinking but a kid who snuck into the party was only 17. He ended up squealing on Mark, and now Mark is charged with giving alcohol to him."

My brothers' reaction was one I did not expect.

"Geez," my brother Tim said. "I thought you were going to tell us you had some serious illness."

My brother Chris added, "Whatever happened to Mark, we're relieved it's only that—and not something bad happening to you." But they had no idea how this was already tearing me to shreds.

■　　■　　■

The upheaval and bizarre turn of events in our lives continued after we returned home from Michigan. Mark and I were unpacking in our bedroom. He turned to me and said, "I'm missing my laptop."

"Your laptop?" I asked. "Your laptop from work?"

"No, my personal laptop," he replied. "I can't find it."

"Do you think you may have left it in the hotel room in Ann Arbor?" I asked. "Should you call the hotel and see if housekeeping found it? If they did, we can have my brother send it back."

Mark called the hotel, but there was no report of a missing computer being found in our room. I called my brother who immediately went to the hotel. The managers explained that they even reviewed security video to see if they could catch any suspicious activity among their staff. Nothing turned up.

It just did not make sense. What I really did not understand is why Mark had not realized he was missing his laptop until we got home. Then again, he had so much on his mind that it could have easily been overlooked.

I never felt more ashamed and humiliated as I did when I returned to the area from Michigan. Perhaps it was partly paranoia, but no matter where I was in public; whether it was walking my dog Molly around Peckville or grocery shopping at the local supermarket, I caught people staring, then whispering, before turning their heads and looking the other way. I felt ostracized in our neighborhood and alienated when I went back to work. It was a horrible feeling trying to save face.

And the anger toward everyone else was building up in me. I supported and defended Mark. I believed him when he told me it was one underage kid who snuck into our home and helped himself to some beer. I was also convinced that the district attorney's office sensationalized the case. Had it been anybody else charged with furnishing alcohol, I thought, it wouldn't have even made the newspaper.

"They are out to get us because of who we are," I kept repeating to friends, family, and co-workers.

My suspicions about the county prosecutors wanting to sensationalize Mark's case became even more apparent when Mark received his official criminal complaint in the mail. The affidavit turned out to be far more incriminating than the account Mark had given me.

When the criminal complaint arrived I sat in Mark's office with him. My own interrogation began.

"The complaint lists people at the party only by abbreviations: C.P., C.G., K.P., L.V., B.H., J.W., M.P., P.S., C.P., AND B.P.," I snapped. "Who are all these people?"

Mark answered, "You don't know them, because they are guys I either know from the gym or I'm helping them with college work."

I suddenly realized that the 17-year-old mentioned in the criminal complaint was related to a family we knew who lived in the same community. But the boy did not live in Peckville. He lived in Scranton.

"How well do you really know this 17-year-old kid?" I asked.

"He may have stopped by once or twice here to see if we needed yard work done," Mark said. "But I never had him do any work around the house."

"But it says you knew him through Facebook?" I argued.

"Honey, there are tons of people I know through Facebook. That doesn't mean anything," Mark responded.

"This (the complaint) says detectives intercepted a picture of you and this kid from that evening?"

"I never posed with that kid," Mark said without skipping a beat. "He was in the background when those pictures were taken. I didn't want him there. I knew how old he was. All the other guys were in college."

"Why didn't you tell me about this party the weekend I took the girls home to moms?" I asked.

"Because to me, it wasn't even a party," Mark answered. "It was just an opportunity to have some of the guys over—and this idiot showed up and threw me under the bus instead of his high school friends that he was out with all night."

More things stood out in the affidavit that seemed like they were thrown in to make Mark look even more sinister but had absolutely no bearing on the case. "The party was the same evening as the Valley View High School Prom." "The boy stated that there was a tap coming out of the wall where they drank the beer from. He believed that they drank an entire keg of Miller Lite from the basement."

I went through the criminal complaint with a fine-tooth comb and continued to drill Mark for a good ten minutes. At the time, I felt more like a reporter than I his wife.

CHAPTER 6

As I was trying to justify Mark's behavior, I was getting angrier with the District Attorney's office. My emotions triggered a phone call to get to the bottom of the misleading information that was in the court papers. I demanded to speak with Gene Talerico, got his voicemail, and left a message. He never returned my call.

Here before me were two very different versions of what happened the night of the party. Mark insisted that this kid showed up, unannounced, yet the county detective investigating the case wrote that he intercepted cell phone pictures of Mark with the boy that evening. I found myself reading the affidavit over and over. I repeatedly asked Mark to recount that evening, begging him to tell me the truth. He never wavered from his original story, which convinced me even more that he was the one being honest about what happened.

. . .

I was standing behind and next to my husband but decided early on that I would not pay for his legal fees. That was up to him to figure out. He got himself into this mess; he would have to get himself out of it. He chose Joe O'Brien, a criminal attorney who worked for the same firm as our attorney and friend who handled the closing of our home. I never asked Mark the total cost of his defense, but I am sure it was not cheap.

It was not long after that Mark agreed to plead guilty to the misdemeanor charge of furnishing alcohol to minors to avoid going to court and further embarrassment. The charge carried a $2,500 fine and up to a year in jail, although Joe O'Brien was confident Mark would avoid jail time since this was his first offense. Up until now, Mark did not even have a traffic violation on his record! Unfortunately, part of the plea deal was that he had to resign from NEIU 19 and surrender all Intermediate Unit resources, including his work laptop. While the worry of living only on my salary was starting to seep into my thoughts, at this point I was more worried about what punishment he would face. If the judge sent him to jail, it would devastate the girls. *Our lives would never be the same,* I thought.

■　　■　　■

If there was anything that worked in our favor, it was that the girls' school year was almost over. I was grateful they did not have to be the object of stares and whispers in the halls by kids who may have seen the news reports. Rachael and Sarah adored their dad. I wanted to try to protect their relationship with and their feelings toward him as much as possible.

After we returned from Michigan, I forced Mark to tell the girls what kind of trouble he was facing. He explained how a 17 year old boy showed up at our house, uninvited, and "got daddy in trouble when this teen told his mom, who then went to the authorities." The girls seemed to take the explanation in stride. Even so, I immediately canceled my subscription to the *Scranton Times-Tribune* in an effort to shield the girls from seeing any articles in the newspaper about their father. I also prohibited the girls from watching television news because Mark's case was on-going. I did not want them to see him being portrayed as a criminal.

I felt good about controlling the information that came into our house. I did not feel good about returning to work. After the Talkback 16 calls and emails, I was reluctant to go back on air.

While not all people do, there are definitely some who revel in other people's hardships. I felt self-conscious and anxious. I knew viewers would be watching my body language and expressions to gauge how I was feeling. They would tune in to see if I would address Mark's legal trouble. It took every ounce of composure and control to act as normal as possible while delivering the news. A sliver of silver lining was that by this time, Mark's charges were old news, so I did not have to worry about his story coinciding with my return to the anchor desk.

Walking into the newsroom that first day back was awkward and intimidating. I felt that management could not or would not look at me in the same way. I sensed that my co-workers really did not know what to say to me or how to say it. It was like approaching someone who had just lost a loved one. When they found the nerve to approach me they usually asked, "how are you doing?" and "how are the girls?" But they never asked how Mark was. I was not forthcoming with the information either. But still, it hurt.

And going live that day was even harder. I tried to report like nothing had happened. On the outside, I was the picture of professionalism. Inside, embarrassment and humiliation had settled deep in my core. So many questions swirled in my mind on a constant loop that I believed my viewers were thinking. Did you know who you married? Why is your husband hanging out with young guys? Did you know what was going on and stayed quiet about it?

Trying to be that consummate anchorwoman was extremely difficult. Banter with my co-anchor, which normally flowed easily, was completely forced. Everything felt so unreal. I was reading the news, but my mind was on how I was going to save face, wondering what people were saying and thinking of me. I felt on the verge of losing myself and my professional identity. I was now learning firsthand what it meant to be living a nightmare.

■　　■　　■

I always looked forward to the last day of school. We used that day to celebrate the girls' academic accomplishments of finishing another year and at the same time rejoice that the summer season was upon us. The girls were dismissed early that day, and Mark decided to take them to the movies to see *Kung Fu Panda* to celebrate.

I decided to leave work early so I could be home when the girls and Mark arrived home after the matinee. It was a warm and sunny day. I was thinking about what to make for dinner and looking forward to spending time together after some very difficult days. But it was not meant to be. Instead of June 6, 2008 being a day to celebrate school being out for summer, it became one of the worst days of my life.

As I was jumping into my car to head home, my phone rang. It was Mark's attorney.

"Marisa? Joe O'Brien. I made arrangements for you to meet Attorney Gerry Karam at his office. You need to meet with him this afternoon. He is waiting for you," he said before I could even manage a hello.

"What is this about?" I asked nervously, suddenly getting that sick feeling in my gut again.

"Well, the district attorney's office hasn't offered any assurances that YOU have been cleared," Joe continued. "It seems as though they believe you knew about what was going on with Mark and they want to talk to you. I can't represent you because I am already representing Mark. Gerry Karam is an excellent criminal defense attorney. He knows you are coming."

Criminal defense attorney, for me? My entire body went numb. *What the hell was going on now?* The DA's office knew the girls and I were not even home when Mark threw that party, and now I was being dragged into this horrible mess?

I drove straight to Gerry's office in downtown Scranton. I had interviewed him for news stories in the past, so we were not total strangers.

"Marisa, good to see you again," he said calmly. "Let's go to my office and I'll fill you in on what is going on."

We sat down. Gerry got right to the point. "It appears Gene Talerico is looking for more information on Mark. He wants to see the both of us in his office this afternoon. But I wanted to see you here first," he said.

"I can't believe they are doing this," I exclaimed with anger. "They just won't give up!"

All I could think of was that a misdemeanor charge was not enough for Talerico. He was looking for something more serious, more sinister, more salacious. I recalled his initial phone call to me when he mentioned "corruption of minors."

Gerry understood my concerns but was careful not to agree with my suspicions about the motivations of the DA's office. "Let's just go ahead and find out what they have to say," he advised.

But I was still defiant.

"Why do I even need a lawyer?" I snapped. "I did nothing wrong. And they continue to blow Mark's trouble way out proportion!"

Gerry assured me that everything would be all right, but that we had to get to the DA's office. When we walked in, I felt as though everyone's eyes were on me. Did they know something I did not know? The anxiety made me tremble more, and my anger was rising. I felt it in my neck and my cheeks. I was sure I was red as a lobster. Gene Talerico was waiting for us in his office and greeted me with a firm handshake. His polite gesture, however, did not subdue my rage. I looked around his office. My eyes landed on a framed picture of a little girl, maybe eight years old. Probably his daughter. I wondered how he would feel if she had to experience the same uneasiness that my daughters were going through.

"Marisa, I asked you here today because I have some more concerns about Mark," he said.

I snapped back, "You mean you haven't done enough damage already? Mark has been charged because of that kid! Had his mom not called you, we wouldn't even be sitting here."

My anger was obvious to both men in the room. Gene seemed to have some compassion and sympathy for what I was dealing with and his words appeared genuine, but at this point I did not trust anyone in law enforcement. Mark had a target on his back, and I feared I would be next. I was in full-on defensive mode and getting angrier by the second. Gene asked Gerry to move to another office so they could talk privately. A few minutes later, Gerry returned alone, and sat down in an armchair next to me, on the opposite side of Gene's desk.

"Well, let me tell you what's going on," Gerry sighed. "The Intermediate Unit (IU) allowed the release of Mark's work laptop to county detectives. The one he handed back to the IU when he resigned."

I had no clue what Gerry was about to share next, but I had a feeling that I was in the path of a train whose brakes had failed. He pulled some photos from an envelope.

"These pictures were confiscated from your husband's work computer," he said, "and some of them have Gene very concerned. He just wants to hear your explanation."

We went through about a dozen photos. Most of them showed young guys swimming in our pool, just horsing around, having fun.

"Do you know any of these guys? Were you ever around when they were swimming in your pool?" he asked. I said no to both questions. Other photos showed guys downstairs in our basement playing air hockey.

Yeah, so what? I thought. I was not sure if the pictures were taken the day Mark had the house party. To me, none of the guys in the photos looked young enough to be in high school, which would legitimize what Mark told me all along – that they were all college-age, with the exception of the one who was 17 years old. There were also family photos- the girls, the girls with Mark and our dog Molly. I looked at Gerry with a blank expression and said nothing.

Gerry continued, "But these are the ones that Gene finds disturbing." He handed me another picture of the girls.

If you ever saw the 1994 movie *Ace Ventura, Pet Detective,* you know there is a very funny scene where Jim Carrey approaches another detective, bends over, bares his bottom, moves the cheeks of his butt with his hands. He then says, "excuse me, I'd like to 'ass' you a question."

The photo Gerry showed me was of the girls, with their pants down, bent over, their bare butts facing the camera, reenacting what they saw Jim Carrey do in the movie. I was there when Mark took the picture in our living room. So was my mother! It was a joke, and we were all laughing. The girls were always trying to be funny. Well, obviously, the DA's office viewed it another way. They interpreted these pictures the way law enforcement does; the photos were perverted, disgusting, and might be considered child porn.

"My mother was there when Mark took these pictures," I exclaimed. "Have Gene call my mother! She can verify all of this! This is absolutely insane! What are they trying to insinuate here?" I felt like the DA's office was throwing everything at me to see what would stick.

Gerry put the photos back into the envelope and started walking out of Gene's office.

"If Gene wants my mother's phone number," I yelled, "I'll be happy to give it to him, so he can call her himself!"

I was so angry at this point that I could hardly breathe. I didn't know whether to continue screaming or start crying. Gerry rolled his eyes as if to indicate that he too could not believe what was happening. He left the office again and returned a few moments later. The news was not good.

"You better get home, Marisa," he advised. "Gene has requested a search of your property."

CHAPTER 7

I practically ran to my car after that meeting. My heart was beating so hard, I thought it would jump right out of my chest. I could hear the *whoosh whoosh* of blood in my ears. Before throwing the car into drive, I grasped the steering wheel. I inhaled and then exhaled heavily. The fear of the unknown was overwhelming. What was waiting for me when I got home? I also knew I needed to calm down before attempting to drive.

As I drove home, I replayed the meeting at the D.A.'s office. How could they not believe me when I explained the picture of the girls? How could they not see it was a misinterpretation? A search of our home! I just could not grasp the reality of this all. I was used to being on the "reporting" side of criminal stories, not the subject of them. Yet, with each passing mile, I was getting closer to learning what it felt like to be on the other side of the news.

I took a deep breath as I approached our neighborhood. It only had one way in and out. A police car was parked at the entrance. I turned onto Blythe Drive and in the distance I saw another cruiser parked in our driveway, about five houses down the street. I shivered as I parked my car in the garage, turned off the engine and headed inside.

As soon as I walked through our laundry room and into the kitchen, I spotted Blakely Police Chief Guy Salerno standing in our center hallway looking like the Swiss Guard. I knew him not only because of my job, but also because the community of Peckville falls within the jurisdiction of Blakely Borough and is therefore patrolled by Blakely police. You know the cops when you live in a small town. I liked his down-to-earth style, and he was a terrific police chief. I always got along with him well. I wanted to treat him nicely now, but it was very difficult to keep my composure.

"Would you mind telling me what is happening here?" I questioned. I sensed that he felt awkward being in my home under these circumstances, that he was just following orders.

"Marisa, I was told to be here to make sure nothing was handled or moved until county detectives arrived," he responded.

I turned around and looked out the sliding French doors in the kitchen where I saw Mark sitting with the girls by the pool. I made a bee line outside.

"Do you know what's happening here?" I asked Mark as I reached to hug the girls. "I was summoned to Gerry Karam's office this afternoon because they found stuff on your work laptop computer. The DA's office is worried about some photos you took. I think they are going to search our home!" I screamed. The girls got upset when they saw me visibly shaking.

"I don't know what they are looking for," Mark responded. "I found out about the search as I was driving home from the movies with the girls." But unlike myself, Mark was unusually calm about what was happening. Maybe he was putting on a good face for the girls. I wanted him to be upset like I was, but he just sat there calm as could be.

"I don't know how much more I can take," I said, a knot forming in my throat.

Moments later, we watched county detectives pull into our driveway. I immediately headed back into the house to wait for the detectives to ring the doorbell. They must have radioed Chief Salerno ahead of time because Guy was already at the front door waiting to let them in. I felt like I was losing control in my own home!

While I met the detectives in the kitchen, Mark stayed outside with the girls. Again, because of my job, I was familiar with detectives Chris Kolcharno and Michelle Mancuso. I knew they investigated child sex abuse cases. And now they were in my home.

The detectives were as polite as could be considering the circumstances. But beyond that, small talk was kept to a minimum. As Chief Salerno continued to stand watch a few feet away, Detectives Kolcharno and Mancuso and I stood around the kitchen table where they explained what was about to happen.

"We've been instructed by the District Attorney's office to search your home because of questionable photos that were found on your husband's work computer," Kolcharno said.

"We can do this one of two ways," Mancuso added, "The investigation is more likely to be kept private and confidential if we are allowed to search without a search warrant—or—we can go to a magistrate, petition the court with probable cause, and obtain a search warrant that way. But if you go that route, the warrant is made public. There's more of a chance that the media will hear about it."

The last thing I wanted was more media attention. I assumed both detectives knew that.

But I have read articles. I have seen news programs, both journalistic and fictional. Law enforcement and the legal system can sometimes be portrayed as presenting cases in a way that may seem far worse than what they really are. As they gather evidence, they throw all they can at a wall to see what sticks. And now, I was living through it-- live and in person.

I was silently cursing the DA's office to hell. How could they be so cruel? Why were they putting my family through this nightmare? And I could just imagine the neighborhood gossip about the police cars in my driveway, especially after the news stories that ran just a few weeks earlier. I was imagining an even bigger ravine opening between us and our neighbors.

At first, I thought finding out about the party and underage drinking was the worst that could happen. Then, I thought it was having the news report on the charges. Then the meeting at the DA's office and the pictures. Now, my home being searched. What would be next?

I was imagining live trucks. Reporters from competitor stations. My WNEP colleagues. All at the edge of our property to report on the breaking news that Marisa Burke's home was being searched! And at this point, I did not even know what for! I assumed the search was to see if there were any other 'questionable' pictures on any other electronic devices in our home, but I really was not sure, and no one had made it clear yet. Not only was I worried about more negative publicity attached to my family, but also how it could possibly end my career at WNEP.

The 'why' was soon revealed. The detectives handed me a Consent to Warrantless Search. My hands were shaking uncontrollably as I read the first few lines:

"We are Detectives Chris Kolcharno and Michelle Mancuso of the Lackawanna County District Attorney's Office. We wish to advise you that you have the absolute right to refuse a warrantless search of the location, 5 Blythe Drive, and that no criminal guilt can be attributed to you for such a refusal. The District Attorney will be searching for evidence, contraband, instrumentalities and fruits of the crime of Sexual Abuse of Children, and that any items seized can and will be used against you or others in a court of law. I fully understand the above and I am willing to, through my legal counsel, consent to the search of my property for the following items: any and all computers, records, documents, cassettes, cartridges, hardware, computer disks, disk drives, flash drives, monitors, computer printers."

The list went on and on.

Then my eyes landed on:

"Any and all books, ledgers and records bearing on the production, reproduction or trading of images of children engaged in a prohibited sexual act as defined by 18 Pa CS 6312."

My God! They are searching to see if we have any child porn on any of our computers!

I assumed the 'probable cause' that led to the search was the picture of the girls with their bare butts in the air; a picture that I insisted was nothing more than just the result of some innocent joking around.

I frantically called both Joe O'Brien and Gerry Karam. Left messages for both. Neither one of them called back. I felt abandoned by the very people who were supposed to help us during this crisis.

My head was spinning. Fearing a magistrate's warrant and the possibility of it being made public, I allowed them to do the search. I was also confident the search would turn up nothing. Child pornography? In our home? Never! I called Mark in from outside because we both had to sign the consent form. As soon as he signed, he went outside again to be with the girls.

I followed the detectives. While they searched and took photos of our home, I stood with my arms folded. With each room we moved through, I became more and more agitated. They carefully disconnected our family computer in the kitchen. They confiscated other electronics as well, including my iPad, digital cameras, even disposable cameras that belonged to the girls. Each item was categorized to keep track of it. Detective Kolcharno asked to see the basement. Again, he snapped photos. Then he noticed the beer tap on the wall in the bar area; the same tap that was mentioned in Mark's affidavit, and he took photos of it.

As someone who treasures privacy, I felt so violated and exposed. I guess I could understand confiscating the electronics to check for anything criminal. But taking all those pictures of my home, both inside and out? What purpose did that serve? I never wanted my home, my private sanctuary, to be on display for anybody. And now I felt as though the house I treasured was a crime scene.

All those years reporting crimes, court cases, and police investigations, and now here I was on the receiving end. *This is what it's like to be suspected of wrongdoing,* I thought. This is what it's like to be "accused." Let me tell you, it's the worst feeling in the world. You feel as though you are the scum of society. The shame of it all hit me like a Mack truck. How would I ever recover from this? Things were a blur. Everything was happening so fast. The circumstances were so surreal.

Believe it or not, however, the worst part of that day was yet to come.

CHAPTER 8

As the detectives categorized the items they had confiscated, I overheard one of them say, "They're on their way."

While I didn't know who the "they" were, I did sense it was going to be yet another step along the road of "how could this possibly get worse?" And boy, it certainly was.

Despite the detectives assuring me that the search and seizure would be kept quiet with no search warrant involved, I did not completely believe them. I worked in broadcast journalism, and I knew people called television stations with "tips." Heck, I received countless calls like that over the years as a reporter, anchor, and news producer. At this point, I was mad enough to wonder if someone in the D.A.'s office would call in the tip.

I became so frantic at the thought of news crews showing up at my door that I seriously considered just getting in my car with the girls and driving far, far away, maybe back to my brother's in Michigan.

Mark was still outside with the girls trying to comfort them under the circumstances. He did his best to try to make them laugh and keep them occupied, but I could tell by the expressions on their little faces that they were scared of these strangers in our house and the police presence in the neighborhood. I stood in the kitchen with the detectives, waiting for the bomb to drop. I did not have the courage to ask them what they meant when they said, "they're on their way." They left as politely as they entered, and I think even one of them even said "good luck with everything." But I learned soon after they left, what they meant when they said, "they're on their way," and it had nothing to do with the media.

Peering out my front window, I watched a woman park up the street. She was walking toward our house. When she reached my door, I opened it up before she rang the bell. She introduced herself and gave me her name. To this day, I cannot recall her name because all I heard was that she was a caseworker-- with Lackawanna County's Children and Youth Services!

"What?" I screamed, "What in the world are you doing here?"

"I'm here at the request of the district attorney's office," she replied very matter-of-factly.

Again, as a broadcast journalist, the only exposure I had to Children and Youth were stories about troubled families or about children in peril because they were being neglected or abused. Whenever you mentioned Children and Youth in a news story it usually suggested something bad, disturbing, or criminal in nature. And now a caseworker was in my home and I feared for what was coming next.

Trying to be polite to her was certainly out of the question. All I wanted to do was rip her apart. I knew that there was no reason for her to be in my home and surmised her presence was based on one photograph. I was furious.

"I have been instructed to make sure your husband leaves this home immediately because the county believes your girls might be in danger," she explained. "I am so sorry about this, but I can't leave until I know your husband is out of the house."

I felt like I was underwater slowly sinking to the bottom, and the farther I drifted from the surface, the more garbled her words became.

The woman anchored herself at our kitchen table, indicating that she would not budge until Mark was gone. She tried to say something empathetic like, "I can only imagine how you feel at this point." But I was having none of it. I glared at her. I was trying to comprehend what was happening, but nothing, absolutely nothing, was making any sense.

I sat down next to her at the table in disbelief. First of all, children and youth agencies are so under-funded and under-staffed, that many times, it takes the agency days to respond to complaints. (I know this because of the constant emails we would receive at Newswatch 16 from families who criticized several different county children and youth agencies for their lack of urgency.) But within a matter of *hours*, Children and Youth showed up at my home, and my children were not in any danger whatsoever! Of course, I thought it was because I was a known public figure. I could imagine the headlines, hear the gossip in the grocery store. I was sinking deeper. *How cold, heartless and calculating the DA's office truly is*, I kept saying to myself, like a mantra. I insisted over and over in my mind that the photo of the girls was totally innocent and done in jest. But I never brought up the photo to the caseworker. I figured she would refuse to listen to anything I had to say anyway. She had her own agenda and she was there on the orders of the DA's office.

The sun was setting, and it was getting cooler out by the pool. Mark brought the girls inside. Rachael and Sarah immediately noticed that the family computer was missing from the desk in the kitchen. This was the computer they used, so they became very upset. They then glanced at the woman, a stranger in their home. Mark was also dumbfounded. Before I had a chance to explain, the caseworker spoke up.

"I am here on behalf of the District Attorney's Office," she said. Then gazing straight at Mark she said, "I'm a caseworker with Children and Youth, and I can't allow you to stay here while there's an ongoing investigation."

I told Mark this was the result of the photo of the girls that they found on his laptop. As much as I was infuriated that the caseworker was in our home, I was finally getting angry at Mark for leaving the photo of the girls on his computer. None of this would be happening had he just stored the image on his personal computer. How could he have been so stupid?

"So the only way this woman will leave our home is if daddy leaves first," I told the girls. I then asked the caseworker how long Mark would have to be away and she really didn't know. "That's up to the district attorney's office," she replied.

I explained to Mark and the girls that if we did not comply with the orders of the DA's office, we might be in serious trouble. The caseworker sat there motionless, looking at the girls, and offering no consolation whatsoever.

"Daddy has to go," I said. At that moment, the girls broke down in tears while Mark just stood there in shock. The prospect of being separated from him was heartbreaking for me and the girls. With his world already crumbling around him, we were basically all he had left; his family was his only hope to go forward.

And now that, too, was being yanked away by a diabolical assistant district attorney.

The caseworker held true to her word. She refused to leave until she saw Mark gather his belongings, get in his car, and drive away. She did not care where he was headed. He just needed to leave. Mark quickly went upstairs and packed a suitcase. I could tell he wanted to get this over with so as not to prolong the agony. He came downstairs, hugged both girls, and kissed them goodbye.

"Everything will be ok girls," he said, trying desperately to hold back tears. "Daddy will be home soon. They'll figure out that this was all a big misunderstanding. I love you both, and daddy will be thinking about you always." At this point, Mark asked the caseworker if he was allowed to talk with Rachael and Sarah over the phone. She said yes. By now, the girls were sobbing hysterically, and I was crying right along with them. It looked like a heart-wrenching scene out of the movies—but this was real. And it involved my family!

After the caseworker witnessed Mark leaving the house and driving away, only then did she gather her purse, a file folder, and her sweater. I escorted her through the laundry room and out through the garage. I returned the kitchen and sat down in a complete daze. Nothing was making sense. I was in total despair.

While Lackawanna County finished its investigation into all the items that were seized from our home, Mark stayed at his parents' home in Scranton where his sister now lived. There was no indication when he would be allowed back home or how that would happen.

How much more could go wrong?

CHAPTER 9

I never told anybody that our home had been raided. Not my colleagues at WNEP, not my friends, not my family. I just could not. The humiliation and shame were unbearable. And then another lightning bolt. Four days after the authorities raided our home, Mark received a letter from Lackawanna County Children and Youth making it official that he was under investigation for possible child abuse. The letter was sent to his sister's house in Scranton because that is where Mark took up residence after he was banished from our home.

The letter was dated June 10. It said a report of suspected sexual child abuse concerning his children and Mark was made to Children and Youth and that under state law, the agency had to investigate to determine whether or not the children were abused. The agency was also required by law to report the suspected abuse to police.

When Mark showed me the letter, I knew he was as shell shocked as I was. How in the world could authorities accuse Mark of sexually abusing our girls based on one silly photo? It was horrifying and disgusting at the same time. I felt like those people who are wrongly accused of a crime, but they are thrown in jail anyway.

As a broadcast journalist, I had reported on these kinds of investigations frequently. And while I always remained professional when presenting the news, in the way-back of my mind, I must admit that I judged and looked down on the people who were accused in cases like these. And now, my husband was being accused of one of the most heinous crimes out there—child sexual abuse. I felt like I was in the middle of a nightmare hoping someone would shake me awake. But instead, I kept getting more and more bad scary news.

The investigation took a few weeks. It felt more like years. During that time, Mark was not allowed at home or to be alone with the girls. And I told no one at work what was going on, not even my boss. I told my mom, brothers, and closest friends as little as possible. I felt on the verge of exploding as I replayed it in my mind on a continuous loop. And each time, I came to the same conclusion. It all looked bad, really bad. I felt like I had to keep it a secret to save face, for the sake of my job, my reputation, and most importantly, to protect the girls.

Anytime that Children and Youth is involved in a case, the word sinister immediately gets stamped on it. And rightfully so, as the agency exists to protect children from abuse. How would it look if it leaked out that someone from Children and Youth was at my house? That my husband was ordered to leave? That he was not allowed to be alone with the girls? I could already hear the TalkBack 16 calls.

Desperately holding on to sanity, I had to keep it together for the sake of the girls, and for the sake of my job. When I was at work, I focused on the task at hand – producing and delivering the news. At home, I focused on staying positive for Rachael and Sarah who were hurt, confused, and scared. But the stress of keeping what was going on a secret from colleagues, family, and friends was taking its toll. I would go days without eating or eating very little. I would manage to swallow a few bites, but then be hit with waves of nausea. I lost 20 pounds. If my close friends and colleagues noticed, they did not say anything or question me about it.

Despite the turmoil surrounding us, Mark, the girls and I were still looking forward to our annual summer vacation to Florida at the end of June. It was the one time during the year we had swaths of time to just hang out at his parents' condo and have fun together free of distractions of daily life and work. And in the summer of 2008, we needed time away more than ever. We already booked our flight, but now we were unsure if Mark would be allowed to go.

I called my attorney, Gerry Karam, to ask to if there would be any issues with Mark leaving the state considering he was not even permitted back into the house. He contacted county investigators who said that Mark would be allowed to go under two conditions:

First, if they found nothing suspicious on any of the electronics they seized from our home.

And second, that I would agree to have the girls interviewed by child advocate investigators and have them examined to see if they had been sexually or physically abused by their father.

As you might imagine, I freaked out over the second condition. "You mean to tell me that I have to have my girls examined as though they were victims of sexual abuse?" I screamed. "This is absolutely insane!"

But Gerry explained that this was part of the investigation and if I did not agree, it would look far worse than it looked right now.

How dare they think that my husband would abuse my girls in any way! What the DA's office was demanding was totally out of line, offensive, and humiliating. I felt as though we were being portrayed as one of those troubled families that I reported about in the news; families that needed intervention because of something seriously wrong. We were far from that, but my hands were tied. The county would not allow us to go to Florida if I did not give in to the request.

I shared all this with Mark via phone while he was staying at his sister's house. He probably felt as though he was stranded on an island. But at that point, I had little pity for him. I was so angry that he put us in this position—even though that photo of the girls was totally innocent. I could tell from the tone of his voice he felt sorry for what the girls and I were going through. But there was little he could do. His hands were tied, too. Talk about feeling helpless.

The Children's Advocacy Center of Northeastern Pennsylvania serves child victims of sexual and physical abuse and neglect. It provides forensic interviews, medical exams, and trauma therapy sessions to young people and their families. But again, while it is meant to be a safe place for children, the thought of having to take my own daughters there brought waves of shame that kept knocking me to my knees.

As much as I protested, I knew there was no way around this. But I did not want anyone to see me go in or out. I did not want to sit in a full waiting room. Since I was worried about being a public, recognizable figure, Gerry helped schedule an appointment in the middle of a workday. I told my boss at work I needed the day off, but I didn't dare tell him the reason.

Leading up to the appointment, I tried to prepare the girls even though I was not really sure about all the details of what would happen. They adored their father and the thought of a father harming his own children was just not in their realm of reality.

"In order for daddy to be allowed to go to Florida, the agency people need to check your private areas," I said, almost choking on the knot in my throat and dumbfounded that I was having this conversation with my 11 and 12-year-olds.

"They will also talk to you for quite some time about whether daddy ever did anything bad to you. For some reason, they think he did, but you know the truth. Just tell the truth."

I contacted the center's executive director, Mary Ann LaPorta, ahead of time to let her know we were on our way.

"I refuse to go through the front door," I insisted to her on the phone. "Do you have a back entrance?"

It was warm and sunny on the day of the appointment. Unlike myself, Rachael and Sarah did not seem annoyed or nervous at all. But I was so angry, I gritted my teeth all the way to Scranton. I went over with the girls one more time on what to expect once they got to the center. All they wanted to know was how long the appointment was going to take because they wanted to get back and swim in the pool.

Mary Ann met us at the back door and immediately tried to put me at ease. "I know how difficult this must be for you, Marisa, but I promise you, the girls will be fine," she said.

Even though she was so polite and compassionate, I snapped, "I don't know why we are here. This is ridiculous." I felt so trapped and so humiliated. Again, Mary Ann tried to calm me down and assured me that the staff would treat the girls just fine.

"This must be Rachael and Sarah," she continued. "My, what lovely girls." She turned to me and said, "Marisa, I made sure that nobody else was here at the center this afternoon, so you have no need to worry about being recognized by anyone."

I was grateful for that.

Perhaps Mary Ann sensed my agony. Perhaps, she could see the rage rising in me. Perhaps, she wanted to help get it over with as quickly as possible. Whatever the reason, she did not prolong the conversation. Instead, she led the girls to the exam rooms. These rooms are used by forensics experts to examine children in sexual abuse cases. I could not believe I was watching my daughters walk into them. They were my baby girls who still played with Barbie dolls. They did not even understand what the "sex" act was because they were too young. As a mother who always protected her children, I felt so helpless, vulnerable, and utterly out of control. I was like a mama bear who perceived her cubs were in danger.

My mind was racing. How were the girls holding up? What were they doing in there? I knew their private parts were being checked, but I had no idea exactly what the exam entailed. Would it be limited to external observation or would there be an internal exam to see if their hymen was broken? Would they become "women" in this cold, clinical setting rather than in a loving experience? Not knowing was tearing me apart. And more so, I felt as though my girls' innocence was being violated. My heart hurt – literally and figuratively.

There I was, a well-known television personality, whose life seemed so perfect, now at a shelter for child victims of sexual and physical abuse, and my girls were being treated as though they were victims! *How could this be happening?* I thought.

Mary Ann tried to occupy me with small talk while the girls were behind closed doors. Some of the conversation was even about WNEP. I may have acknowledged that she was there, but for the most part, I tuned her out. It was just so surreal that I was in a place like this, having my girls examined like they were grown women at an ob-gyn appointment.

As soon as the girls came out of the exam rooms, they were whisked upstairs to be interviewed. I did not have a chance to talk to either of them.

A worker sat down next to me to explain what would happen in the interviews. She may have told me her name, but I was in such a state, I fail to remember. The memory of that afternoon was blurry, like I was looking at it through a rain-soaked window. I do remember she assured me that there would be no leading questions to trap the children and force them to say something that might incriminate themselves or Mark.

"We uphold integrity, sanctity, and confidentiality," she promised.

I was too blind with rage to believe her.

I sat with my arms folded the whole time the girls were being interviewed. I felt like the minutes were ticking by in slow motion, like I could hear the click of an old-fashioned clock as each minute turned over into the next. My mind was on my girls. I knew they were being interviewed separately. I wondered what they were thinking, what they were feeling. Every so often, Mary Ann would try small talk again to see how I was doing. But I still was not interested in talking to anyone. My rage and frustration were boiling. Sitting there felt like an eternity, but in reality, the exams and interviews took less than an hour.

When Sarah and Rachael walked back into the waiting room, they looked unfazed and did not appear to be nearly as upset as I was. They seemed more interested in getting home and jumping in the pool than talking about what had just happened.

During the drive home, the girls shared very few details about the physical exam and offered little information about the interviews, except for one detail. As much as I was promised that the interviews would not consist of leading questions, the girls told me that the woman who interviewed them asked, "You know your father has a problem, don't you?" If that wasn't a leading question, I don't know what is.

CHAPTER 10

I was confident from the beginning that investigators would not find anything unlawful on any of the electronics seized from our home on June 6th. And even though they never outright said they did not discover anything Mark was given permission to fly to Florida that month because the child abuse investigation also turned up nothing. We received this letter dated June 19:

Dear Mr. & Mrs. Kandel:

We are writing to inform you that the child abuse investigation on Rachael and Sarah Kandel has been determined to be unfounded. In other words we were not able to prove that the children were abused. All records on the case will be destroyed within one year + 120 days.

Right there in black and white. The Children's Advocacy Center failed to gather any incriminating evidence after the girls' examinations and interviews. For the first time in a while I felt vindicated. I wanted to send it to the DA's office and call Gene Talerico. I wanted to scream, "See what you put us through for nothing?" I wanted him to rot in hell.

■   ■   ■

I could not pack our bags fast enough. I could not wait to get miles between us and northeastern PA; between us and the news and whispering people in the grocery store. I could not wait to get my feet in the sand, see the calm waters of the Gulf, and breath in salty air.

Florida and the condo that Mark's family owned felt like a refuge that summer because it was a place where no one recognized us; a place where we were not subjects of the 6 o'clock news. And for the first time in weeks, I not only could think about eating, I could actually enjoy it. The vacation was heaven, until the last few days.

We were enjoying dinner on the beach at one of our favorite restaurants, one where we always make reservations at a time when we can watch the amazing sunset over the Gulf. After we finished eating, the girls went down by the surf to search for shells. Mark and I kept an eye on them from our table.

My phone rang. It was my brother Tim.

"Did you happen to see what the Scranton newspaper reported today?" he asked.

My stomach turned over.

"I haven't been reading or watching any news down here," I replied. "I really don't want to know what's going on back home while I'm on vacation. I really needed a break from it all."

There was a pause.

Then, Tim continued, "Well, you know that boy who got Mark in trouble? It sounds like investigators found a text from Mark on the kid's cell phone, and it isn't good. Mark apparently asked this kid about how he grooms his private parts. It's pretty graphic, and it's all in this article."

The panic was rising. I glared at Mark.

"The article also said your house was searched earlier this month," Tim said. "Marisa, was your house raided?"

I sat there speechless, and again in a state of shock. Mark's eyes were now fixated on me, wondering who was on the phone and what they were saying.

"I've got to go," I told my brother, "we'll talk later."

With my voice quivering and my body shaking, I told Mark what my brother said was in today's newspaper.

"Is this true?" I asked him.

Mark responded that the context of his text was just locker room humor and nothing more.

"All guys talk like that," he countered. "Ask anybody. They'll tell you the same thing."

"Then why is it in the paper?" I snapped.

"Honey, I have no idea," he answered.

We sat there for a few minutes going back and forth, finally convincing ourselves that, once again, it was the DA's office out to attack and embarrass us. The office knew we were out of town so what better time to leak this to the newspaper. Besides that, I quickly realized we were lied to when the detectives said the search of our home would be kept under wraps if we agreed to it, which we did. At this point, it was also quite clear to me that the D.A.'s office was not giving up until prosecutors found the salacious evidence they were looking to find.

I was livid. I looked out at the girls near the water. Picking up shells. Consulting each other about which ones to keep and which to toss. Laughing. This vacation had been such a salve for me, for our family. A time to step away from the real world. And now this bombshell.

We went back to the condo after dinner, and I tried to keep a happy face for the girls. I did not want them to know what my brother told me. And again, Mark seemed unfazed by the news, like he was with the photo of the girls, as if showing confidence would help him beat this latest embarrassment as well.

The next day when I was sunbathing by the pool, I called Gene Talerico. I left several messages, but he never called me back. At the same time, I learned from some of my work friends that Newswatch 16 also ran stories, most of them leading the newscasts, with the new information about Mark and about the seizure of items from our home. The script that aired on June 20, 2008:

{**ANCHOR**}

We're learning more about an investigation into a man accused of providing alcohol to minors at a party last month in Lackawanna County.

{**ANCHOR**}

The Lackawanna County District Attorney says investigators seized digital cameras and computers from Mark Kandel's home in Peckville a few weeks ago.

Until recently, Kandel worked at the Northeast Educational Intermediate Unit. Detectives are also looking at evidence seized from his office as well.

5PM 6/20/2008
{**ANCHOR**}

New details are emerging tonight in the investigation of an underage drinking party in Lackawanna County. The District Attorney says investigators seized computers and digital cameras from the home of Mark Kandel. Kandel, who resigned from the Northeastern Educational Intermediate Unit, was charged with providing alcohol to minors last month. Authorities say the party happened here at Kandel's home in Peckville and that they learned some of the details from text message Kandel allegedly sent to a 17-year-old boy. Kandel's next court appearance is in July.

6PM 6/20/2008
[TOP STORY]
{**ANCHOR**}

New details about an underage drinking case involving a former worker with the Northeastern Educational Intermediate Unit.

{**ANCHOR**}

The latest on the investigation into Mark Kandel is our top story on Newswatch 16 at 6.

Good evening. Kandel, until recently, worked for the NEIU. He's accused of giving alcohol to minors during a party at his home earlier this year. Newswatch 16s Josh Brogadir is live in the newsroom with the latest on the investigation. Josh?

[JOSH LIVE IN NEWSROOM]

Authorities in Lackawanna County say Kandel voluntarily turned over evidence to the D-A's office. And following the initial investigation last month, detectives are learning more about this case.

[VIDEO STORY]

New information has surfaced in the investigation into an underage drinking party last month at this home in Peckville, Lackawanna County. The DA says investigators seized digital cameras and computers a few weeks ago that belonged to Mark Kandel. The 48-year-old former Scranton school board director was charged with providing alcohol to 11 people under the age of 21 at a party at his house in May. Authorities were tipped off by the mother of a 17-year-old who says she saw text messages on her son's phone. After that, investigators say they recorded text messages and a phone conversation between Kandel and the teenager. Kandel later resigned his position at the Northeastern Education Intermediate Unit #19, a job he had for about five years. Officials there say he gave presentations to educators on staff development and continuing education.

(Josh Standup)

"The executive director told Newswatch 16 Kandel walked into his office and resigned last month. The NEIU then turned over Kandel's computer at the request of the district attorney."

The DA declined to talk on camera due to the ongoing investigation but said after the initial investigation into the party last month, he became aware of additional information involving Mark Kandel.

[JOSH LIVE IN NEWSROOM]

Mark Kandel was not at his home when we stopped by today. His next court appearance is scheduled for July.

Josh Brogadir, Newswatch 16, live in the Newsroom.

So much for a seizure being kept private. It was all over the news and now the entire viewing area knew we had a raid at our home! *The DA's office had every intention of leaking this out to make us look bad, to make us look suspicious,* I angrily said to myself. The shame and embarrassment mingled with a feeling of betrayal. It was not the kind of cocktail I normally liked, and it went down hard and bitter.

Returning to work after our vacation was dreadful to say the least. No one in the newsroom had the right words to say to me, so they kept their distance. I wanted and needed some consoling, but there was none. Even though the station had broadcast the story about Mark a few days before my return, everyone just went about their business, pretending that everything was completely normal. I dove into organizing my desk and catching up on emails before the newsroom morning meeting. Out of the corner of my eye, I saw Erik Shrader, the news director, casually walking over to my desk.

"How was your vacation?" he asked. And before I could even respond he continued, "Hey, can I see you for a moment?"

I was not surprised. I assumed he would have questions and expect answers from me. My stomach started to somersault. I stood up assuming we would meet in his office. But instead of leading me there, he said, "follow me," and we headed toward the administrative side of the building. It suddenly became obvious that station executives would be involved in the conversation. This was not good. My heart pounded.

I will answer their questions honestly and clarify what I can, I thought. Then just head back to my desk and continue with my workday. It took everything I had to keep my composure. Bob Hawkins, the station's controller, met us in the sales conference room. He explained that he was sitting in for the general manager who was called out of town on a family emergency.

The conversation began with them reminding me that even though I was not accused of any wrongdoing, I was still Mark's wife, and therefore, linked to his trouble. They made it very clear that WNEP management could not put the station's reputation in jeopardy and that they were getting nasty emails about Mark and my connection to him. I could feel my face turning red.

They were especially annoyed that I had not told them our home was raided and electronics confiscated. By not saying anything, it gave the impression that I was hiding something. My heart was racing. I took a deep breath. When it was my turn to speak, I defended Mark and repeated that I believed he was the victim of a prosecutorial witch-hunt. The looks on their faces showed they were skeptical. My news director then suggested I take a leave of absence at least until after Mark's scheduled hearing in July.

"Considering what was reported in the newspaper while you were gone, and the fact that it seems more and more information is coming out about Mark's investigation, we think it would be wise if you took some time off to be with your family," Erik said.

I knew immediately this had nothing to do with 'spending time with my family,' but instead it was a matter of distancing me from WNEP. That way, if more bombs dropped, I would already be off the air.

Up until now, whenever there was an update to report about Mark's case, like an upcoming hearing, management allowed me to take a few days off to avoid the awkward position of anchoring the news. But this was different. It felt different. I was being told to take several weeks of leave. All along I thought my coveted position and status at WNEP was untouchable. But I thought wrong. What a blow to my pride and my self-esteem! And it just proved that no one in the news business is indispensable.

I reluctantly agreed to take a paid leave of absence and to sign a legal document promising to keep station management in the loop of any new developments concerning Mark and substantiating that I had no knowledge of him allegedly serving alcohol to minors.

The following is WNEP-TV's detailed account of our meeting that day as well as the declaration I signed. Both documents were put in my personal file and are probably still in the station's records:

A meeting was conducted with Marisa Kandel on Wednesday 6/25 at approx. 9:45am in the sales conference room. The meeting lasted approx.. 45 minutes ending at 10:30am. In attendance were Marisa Kandel, Erik Schrader and Bob Hawkins. Bob started the discussion on a light note asking Marisa how her vacation was. Erik informed Marisa that Lou Kirchen was unable to attend this meeting due to a family emergency that led to her being out of town. Erik then moved the conversation to asking Marisa if she and her daughters were ok. Marisa responded by stating that she was grateful that they were away when the recent allegations were made. The discussion then turned to the importance of Marisa's honesty in this situation and how important it was for there not to be any more surprises. Erik asked Marisa why she had not informed us of the seizing of Mark's computer, and she stated that she was only acting on her attorney's advice. She continually stated that there had not been any more charges in this case and that she felt that the Assistant District Attorney was trying to take Mark down and it would be even better for him if he took Marisa down also. She stated that he is always trying to take the "big fish" out. She stated that the ADA has let the information out that was printed in Friday's newspaper since he could not get Mark on any other criminal charges and that these incidents were not criminal in nature. At this point, Erik asked Marisa if she thought it would be a good idea if she were to take a leave until this situation resolves itself. Bob offered that she had approx. 3 weeks of unused leave remaining which would take her just about to Mark's hearing date of 7/23/08. Erik also mentioned that Lou Kirchen may approve an additional week if we felt that this was in the best interest of both Marisa and the station. Marisa responded by stating that she was unsure if this was a good idea and wanted to think about it for a while. Erik informed her that we could not wait too long for this decision since we needed to cover that evenings newscast. She then asked if she would be able to stay at work and continue to produce the newscast to which Erik told her that he did not think that was a good idea. Both Erik and Bob discussed with her how challenging that could become if something else would break in this incident. At this point Marisa was asked if she felt anything else would develop in this case to which she stated she did not think so but "who knows". Marisa then stated that it was very difficult for her to walk into the building this morning worried about the opinions of her co-workers. At that point, Erik mentioned that "parties" at her house have been a topic of discussion around the building and that we were very concerned about them. She became very defensive at that point and stated that the last big party at her house was one of her friend's engagement parties and that it certainly did get out of hand. Bob then stated that the stories we were hearing were just rumors as far as we were concerned. Marisa then stated that the recent parties at her house (ones that both Mark and I hosted) did not involve any one at work. Marisa then mentioned that maybe a leave would be appropriate. At this point, Bob presented Marisa with the "Declaration" that was drafted by the company's attorney. Marisa reviewed the document and immediately signed it without any reservation. Bob took the agreement and made an additional copy for Marisa. Marisa then expressed her concern in regards to the newspaper reports that the party that Mark allegedly hosted was not a "prom party" and that they were having this removed from the record. She repeatedly stated that these individuals showed up at her home "unannounced". Marisa stated that Mark was going to the DA's office today in hopes of having his hearing moved up and that now her situation at work would have an effect on that. Both Bob and Erik continue to remind Marisa that we could not jeopardize the reputation of the station and that by her signing the "Declaration" she would be required to keep us informed of any developments and she nodded in agreement. The meeting ended and Marisa went back to her desk and gathered a few items and left the building.

DECLARATION

Marisa Burke Kandel makes the following declaration:

1. I was not aware of the party which allegedly took place in May 2008 at my home allegedly involving my husband serving alcohol to minors which is the subject of a criminal investigation.

2. I did not attend the party referred to in paragraph 1.

3. I was not aware of any emails which my husband allegedly sent to minors that are the subject of the aforementioned criminal investigation.

4. I agree that I will keep WNEP-TV fully and timely informed of all matters related to the criminal investigation that are or may become known to the public and are not legally privileged.

5. I understand that complying with the foregoing declaration is a condition of my employment.

I hereby make the above declaration freely and voluntarily.

CHAPTER 11

When I left the meeting with my news director and the station's controller, I walked back down the long hallway to the newsroom, headed straight for my desk, picked up my belongings I brought for the day, and scurried out the door. I tried not to make eye contact with anyone. I refused to speak to anyone. I was too embarrassed to try to strike up a conversation with any of my co-workers. I figured they would either find out what was going on with me through conversations with the news director or by mass email. At this point, I did not care. I just wanted to get home. But I could not help but think, *is this my fall from grace? Was this the end of my career at the station?* My spirit was broken, and all of this was not even my fault. The rejection I felt driving home was so unbearable that all I wanted to do was hide from everyone. How would I explain my absence from the air to my mom, who lived every day to watch me on TV? What would I say to my brothers and my friends? I was now on a hiatus from the job I lived for and loved.

Broadcast news was the one constant I still had in my life after all this chaos, and now I felt like it, too, was quickly fading away in the rear-view mirror. The biggest fear I had was not knowing if the break from my job was really temporary, or if WNEP would decide to make it permanent. Mark's trouble was affecting me in so many different ways, emotionally and personally, and now it was affecting my job, my career, everything I worked so hard for all these years.

My eyes were filled with tears when I walked through the door at home. Rachael and Sarah greeted me with surprise and said, "Mommy, what are you doing home?" Mark was within an earshot, but I spoke directly to the girls.

"My bosses thought that with everything going on with daddy, that I should have some time off. So I'm going to be home for a while," I said.

The girls looked at me, then looked at each other, before turning back to me, jubilantly screaming, "This is fantastic! You're going to be home this summer!"

As dejected and depressed as I felt at that moment, the girls rejoicing about me being home during their summer vacation buoyed me. My unexpected leave of absence was also comforting to Mark who was looking for my support and reassurance that, together, we just might have enough fortitude to forge through this horrible ordeal.

"This is great, honey, that you'll have some time off for a while," Mark said. But I took him aside and told him the conversation I had with Erik and Bob emphasizing their displeasure that I avoided telling them about the raid at our home and that they had to read it in the newspaper. I added that they were also upset with the new information that Mark dismissed as 'locker room humor.' I wanted him to know that at this point I was not sure if I even had a future at WNEP. Mark stayed silent. No reaction to what I had said. No comforting reassurance.

In the moment, it was hard to see the leave as anything but punishment. But looking back, perhaps it was divine intervention. Maybe it was a gift. I was handed six weeks during the summer to be at home with my family. The summer of 2008 was hot and sunny, which allowed us to be outside and in the pool most of the time. I also now had time to cook dinner and loved being home with my family. We spent most evenings playing games or watching a movie together. The girls were in paradise because they were with mommy and daddy all the time.

This "bonding" time together as a family was solidified even more because I had gone into seclusion. Having privacy became the upmost priority. I cut ties with so many things that connected the girls and me with the outside world. No more subscriptions to newspapers. Internet browsing was impossible because the girls' computer had been confiscated. I had our land line disconnected. With the exception of a few close girlfriends, I cut off communicating with most friends, co-workers, and even family members. They would call and leave messages, but I did not call back. It was almost as though I had built this great big imaginary wall around us. My reclusive behavior allowed me to put up my guard and provided me with the strength I needed to protect the girls and me from any further emotional damage.

When I look back now, I should have gone to therapy. Processing what was happening with a trained professional probably would have helped me move through the ordeal more easily than the manner in which I was coping. But the thought of seeing a therapist never crossed my mind at the time.

One day when I was looking for a sympathetic ear, I reached out to a very dear friend who was a Roman Catholic priest. I was sitting in a rocking chair on our front porch alone. I do not even remember where Mark and the girls were. But I was alone and in a reflective mood. So I called this friend hoping he would offer some words of wisdom after everything I had been through. No answer. A few minutes later I called again, and this time I left a voicemail. I left several voicemails after that day, but he never returned any of my calls. I never heard from him again.

That same day, I also reached out to my mother. She answered the phone, but her reaction was disturbing just the same. We started our conversation by catching up on the girls and how they were enjoying their summer. I told her it was wonderful being with them during my leave. Then our conversation turned to Mark. I took a deep breath. "He will be pleading guilty when he's in court again at the end of July," I told her.

Instead of asking how Mark and I were doing, and instead of offering words of compassion and concern, she said, "I just don't know how all of this is going to look to my friends." Her comment hurt me beyond belief.

My mother Maria grew up in Shenandoah in the heart of the coal region in Pennsylvania. Her parents separated when she was in high school, and she stayed with her mother. They did not have much, but my mother did attend college – the first in her family to do so. After she graduated from Immaculata College near Philadelphia, she accepted a job as a microbiologist at a pharmaceutical company in the Danville area. (After she had my brothers and me, she earned a teaching certificate and taught the rest of her career.) She met my father at the only Catholic church in town.

My father James had been born and raised in Danville. He did not attend college, but still was able to become a banker. People often compared him to George Bailey in *It's A Wonderful Life* because he was so genuine and caring. And like George, more times than not, he tried to help people however he could, even if they did not have the financial means on paper.

My parents built a comfortable life for themselves out of almost nothing. They were proud of what their careers had given us, and they took immaculate care of the Cape Cod home they lived in their entire married life. They were active in the community. Growing up, I watched and learned. I absorbed their beliefs, values, and work ethic. I admired them.

I also grew to learn that appearances mattered to my mother. She worried about what others said and thought. And hearing that in her comment was like a dagger in my heart. For the rest of the summer, I distanced myself from my mother. I needed time and space. I would not answer her calls, and I refused to visit her.

While I did find strength in isolating from family and friends, there were a few close friends, not associated with WNEP, who I would invite to sit by the pool on some of those warm summer evenings. We sipped wine, shared conversation, and shed tears. Our discussions centered on how Mark was being so unfairly mistreated by prosecutors. They always seemed to completely agree with me and always offered genuine concern and sympathy. I trusted them with my soul. They know who they are, and I will always be very grateful to have them in my life.

■　　■　　■

Mark was scheduled to plead guilty July 25th in Lackawanna County Court. Even though the sentencing guidelines called for up to a year in jail for furnishing alcohol to minors, Mark tried to convince me that sort of punishment was not likely because this was a first criminal offense against him. *But what if the judge sentences him to jail time, even if it is for six months?* I thought. It would be devastating for the girls and absolutely horrible for me.

I knew his court appearance would turn into a media circus especially if I were there, so for spite, I did not go with him. His sister Kim went instead. Mark courageously left the house that morning dressed impeccably in a handsome suit and tie, hair slicked back, carrying a black portfolio case. He looked like he just walked out of a Brooks Brothers catalog.

Once again, I refused to watch the news that day, as I never wanted the girls to see their father on TV. But later I received a full account from both Mark and his sister. Mark did not shield his face from cameras the way many defendants do going in or out of court. But he did purposely wear sunglasses on his way out of the courthouse so no one could see his eyes. News photographers hate that because the eyes can show so much emotion. Kim described how they both barreled their way right through the media mob—nearly knocking down some of them. I found that amusing and actually gave them both kudos for storming past and refusing to answer any of questions. Even so, Mark's court appearance to plead guilty to one count of furnishing alcohol to minors ended up again being the lead story on Newswatch 16 at 6 p.m.:

[**ANCHOR**]

A former Scranton school director pleaded guilty today to providing alcohol to minors in Lackawanna County. Newswatch 16's Josh Brogadir has the story:

[video story]

Mark Kandel, seen here walking with his sister, did not comment to reporters on his way in or out of the Lackawanna County Courthouse this morning. His day in court was scheduled as a pre-trial hearing, but the former Scranton school director who worked until May at the Northeastern Educational Intermediate Unit #19 instead pleaded guilty to one count of providing alcohol to minors. Investigators say the 48-year-old hosted a party for teenagers back in May at his house in Peckville, and that he served them beer and liquor. Authorities were tipped off by the mother of a 17-year-old boy who says she saw text messages on her son's phone. After that, investigators say they recorded text messages and a phone conversation between Kandel and the teenager.

We asked authorities today if computers and a digital camera seized as part of the investigation had been returned to Kandel but they would not say, nor would they comment on any ongoing investigation.

{Gene Talerico/First A.D.A. Lackawanna County}

"At this point we're not commenting on whether the case is open or closed other than to say that this portion of the case is complete."

{Josh Brogadir/Newswatch 16}

"Mark Kandel's attorney declined to comment. Kandel faces up to a year in prison and a 25-hundred dollar fine. He will likely be sentenced in the next 90 days. Josh Brogadir, Newswatch 16, Scranton."

Mark was surprisingly calm when he finally returned home that day. At the same time, I was super angry at Gene Talerico for insinuating in his media interviews that Mark could still be facing trouble if they found anything suspicious on the electronics they had seized from our home the month before. As if to imply, "stayed tuned folks, there's more to come." But we already knew that had investigators found anything suspicious, Mark would not have been allowed to go to Florida in June.

■　　■　　■

The weekend after Mark's guilty plea, we took the girls to Hershey Park with my friend Jacqueline (Jackie) Frank and her family. The girls were close in age with her sons, and they always had a good time together. We were walking around the park as the children went from one roller coaster to another when my cell phone rang. It was my news director. "Marisa, now that Mark's hearing is over, we were wondering if you could come back to work," he asked.

When my leave of absence began, management never spelled out exactly when I would return to work or in what capacity. Heck, for that matter, I was not even sure if I had a job to return to! And to be honest, I was not totally convinced I was prepared to go back on the air and anchor the news like nothing happened.

But as I sat there on a bench in the middle of Hershey Park, my boss argued why it would be best for me to return to work and guaranteed that no one in the newsroom thought any less of me.

"Thank you so much for calling," I said. "And thank you for being so understanding during this time. I appreciate the leave of absence but I'm ready to get back to work."

That following Monday, I went back on the air. Despite what they thought about Mark, my co-workers were cordial, attentive, and extremely respectful. It took me a few evenings to get back into the groove of being back on air while also trying to keep an "everything's fine" face.

Just a few weeks after I returned to work and a month before Mark's sentencing, my co-anchor, Mike Lewis, abruptly left WNEP. I had not seen his departure coming, and in a strange way, it made me feel vulnerable. Even though we had gotten off to a rocky start when he first joined the WNEP team, we had overcome our differences and learned how to work together like two pieces of the puzzle. And now someone had pulled the puzzle apart. Mike brought me work security and consistency, which I desperately needed during this uncertain time in my personal life. And now that was gone, too.

■　　■　　■

Weeks went by without any word from the district attorney's office about the items taken from our home in June. We were still without the family computer, school was about a month away, and I finally said, *enough is enough.* Even I knew that it did not take months for a forensic examination of electronics. And I knew that if investigators had found anything incriminating, we would have certainly heard about it by now. So, instead of calling, I paid a visit to the district attorney's office.

The only physical contact I ever had with the district attorney's office was on a professional basis, mainly for news stories that involved some sort of criminal case. This time however, I was headed there as a regular citizen to demand the return of our possessions. I drummed up enough courage to walk through the front door of the office in downtown Scranton and marched right up to the thick glass window that securely separated office staff from visitors. A woman greeted me on the other side of the window. "My belongings were taken from my home back in June and I'm here to collect everything they took," I said sternly. She obviously recognized who I was and said, "one moment please."

Within minutes someone else walked into the waiting area and handed me a box. I wanted so much to make a scene. I wanted to yell and scream and say *you made a big fuss seizing all our belongings and leaking the raid at our home to the news media about it. But now that you didn't find anything, you're silent! Where the news conference now?*

The person offered to help me to my car to which I angrily responded, "No thanks. I'd much rather do it myself." I felt a sense of empowerment as I shoved that box into the trunk of my car but remained frustrated. They had made such a big deal when they took all this stuff, but they certainly did not inform the media when nothing was found on it. Again, it reinforced my on-going suspicion of a prosecutor's motivation to bring down Mark and me.

■ ■ ■

In the weeks leading up to Mark's sentencing in October, several people offered to write letters to the judge on Mark's behalf.

An excerpt from the letter written by the Senior Warden at the Church of the Good Shepherd, Warren Shotto, read as follows:

Mark works in tandem with the clergy and lay leadership to ensure that all aspects of the faith are instilled in the future generations. I can confirm that he is a man of integrity and is extremely dedicated to his family and work. He has worked tirelessly for the church, as well as community organizations, like Serving Seniors and Family to Family, to aid those who struggle and are less fortunate.

Mark and his family have been leaders, role models and stalwart supporters, not only of the Church of the Good Shepherd for generations, but of its parishioners as well. He is someone on whom we can always count and is held in high regards, both professionally and personally.

And here is an excerpt from the letter written by my close friend Jackie who was also a former graduate student of Mark:

I first met Dr. Kandel at Marywood University when I was a graduate student. He was my professor and cooperating teacher. I found him to be a highly-motivated, hard-working, and committed educator.

Mark is a loyal, honest, and considerate individual who I would trust implicitly with my children. He has, on countless occasions, helped me when I was in a bind with babysitting, professional issues, and personal problems.

Mark's family is what is most important to him. He is the quintessential "hands on" dad, and his daughters positively adore him. His wife's erratic work schedule has positioned him in the role of primary caregiver to his girls. He is home when they get off the bus; he makes them a home-cooked meal every night; he takes them to swimming and chorus practice, and makes sure that their homework is always completed. It is worth noting that Mark's presence in his family is vital to the stability and emotional well-being of his children.

Even though his life was turned upside down, Mark never stepped back from his fatherly role and responsibilities for Rachael and Sarah. He was always there to drive them to where they needed to be, whether it was to a friend's house or swim meets. As their lives got busier with homework and after-school activities, he was right there for them. And he still managed to make us laugh everyday with his jokes, impersonations, and innate quick wit. He was now looking for employment, but at the same time, helping me as much as he could with chores around the house while I continued to put in long days at work. We tried to act as normal as possible but his sentencing date in October was now weeks away and the anticipation, along with the anxiety, was gnawing at me. We rarely had sex anymore. We were more like a brother and sister than we were husband and wife. But again, I chocked it up as stress from his criminal case and my intense schedule at work. And yet, I felt it was my responsibility and duty to support him for the sake of our family's survival. I tried like anything not to lose confidence in the days leading up to his sentencing, but I really did not have a good feeling about the outcome.

Mark left the courthouse after he was sentenced and came straight home. He walked into the kitchen where I was trying to keep myself busy. He managed to smile a bit, but I could tell he was stressed out. Perhaps all of the anxiety was finally starting to take its toll. "Well, I guess it could have been a lot worse," he said. It turned out the judge sentenced him to 90 days of house arrest followed by nine months of probation.

"Well, you'll be going into the holiday season tied to the property," I responded. "This year, maybe you can help me decorate." We both sort of chuckled to try to blanket the pain we were both feeling.

On October 20, 2008, *The Scranton Times-Tribune* reported that Mark was sentenced to 90 days house arrest for providing alcohol to minors at our home and that he would be placed on house arrest in mid-November. But in the lead line of the story, it mentioned that he was the husband of WNEP's Marisa Burke. Another gigantic wave of humiliation hit me like a tsunami and there was no running away from it. The article went on to state that after Mark's house arrest he would remain on probation for another nine months. No teenagers were allowed in our home without permission from the court. And Mark was not allowed to have any alcohol or go to any restaurants that served alcohol.

I guess I should have been relieved at the punishment Lackawanna County Judge Michael Barrasse imposed on Mark that day. After all, he escaped serving time in jail. Desperately trying to find a silver lining, I thought, how bad could house arrest be? But it was difficult to ignore some of the backlash after Mark was sentenced. Some thought he got off too easy. The gaining popularity of social media in 2008 allowed people to voice their hurtful comments using all sorts of forums. One such blog was called *Northeast PA media news and gossip*. Here are just some of the comments that were posted after Mark's sentencing:

Anonymous said: "This was a case of rich man's justice. He got a sweet deal from the judge, and he had the nerve to hide his face on his way out of the courthouse. I hope the families of the victims whack Kandel and Burke with a civil suit. That'll wipe the smirk off his face."

Anonymous said: "Wow. More like rich white man's justice. His parties were like that scene in Gods and Monsters only the attendees were younger."

Anonymous said: "Talk to anyone who lives in the neighborhood. I have. That party was not a one-time thing. It's been going on for years. In the summer, it's out by the pool, young men cavorting to and fro."

Anonymous said: "Mark Kandel is a good guy if you know him. I think all you people are touched. I bet anyone else that had a m3 misdemeanor wasn't all over the newspaper and news you people need to get a life."

The thing about social media? People can post whatever trash they want with generally no repercussions and do it anonymously. I always thought these were the cowards. If you are so intent on spreading lies and misinformation, then why don't you have the guts to leave your name on your post? Regardless of the nasty emails and online posts, WNEP excused me from work the day Mark was sentenced so I could avoid the awkwardness of being on air while the story was being broadcast. Granted, most of our viewers were sympathetic to me and my girls, but very few felt sorry for Mark. And that is what hurt. They failed to see the good man, the devoted husband and the loving father the girls and I were fortunate to be around every single day. They only saw the bad.

CHAPTER 12

"Karma.
No need for revenge.
Just sit back and wait.
Those who hurt you will eventually screw up themselves and if you're lucky,
God will let you watch."
~Dharam Sherathia

By December 2008, Mark had an ankle bracelet that tracked his whereabouts. He could leave to do errands, pick up the girls, go to church, and for appointments. But every time he left the house, he had to contact his probation officer. If he did not, the bracelet would send an alert. And he was not allowed to leave the state (or country) during his house arrest. Not that we had any travel plans. Mark and I rarely talked that much about his restrictions or the ankle bracelet. He sometimes made jokes about it, and I would laugh. But that was it. And honestly, as long as he was still able to take the girls where they needed to go, and it did not interfere with my work, I figured I could tolerate the 90-day house arrest. It was temporary, and I focused on that. Really, I had no choice.

During this time, the teenager, who was the center of Mark's criminal case made the news. This time, Mark was not a part of the story. Now 18-years-old,

Marisa Burke

the young man was in a serious car crash on a rural road. He and his four passengers were injured. Investigators determined alcohol was involved.

As much as I felt badly about people getting hurt, I saw this crash as proof that this young man was trouble from the very beginning. Here's a person who I felt ruined my husband's career, and who was now facing criminal charges of his own.

At last, some vindication for Mark, I rejoiced to myself. My mistake was I did not leave well enough alone.

My obsession with this kid's case wrongly turned into revenge. As it moved through the legal system, I pressed my colleagues at Newswatch 16 to air every aspect of it.

"This is the kid who got my husband in trouble," I purposely mentioned to a few key people in the newsroom. "What goes around, comes around, I guess."

But my comments made their way back to newsroom managers, who I presumed suspected my agenda. From that moment on, the editorial staff used discretion on how much attention to give the crash story and the repercussions from it.

Day in, day out, my thoughts were the same; I wanted to get even with this guy after what he put my husband through. I even wrote letters to the DA's office pointing out that its case against Mark was based on this kid who ended up breaking the law and seriously injuring others.

"Where's the justice now?" I questioned in these letters.

But my pernicious behavior did not end there. I called the police chief who handled the drunk driving case encouraging him to throw the book at this kid. South Abington Police Chief Robert Gerrity was someone I always respected because of his 'street smarts.' We always had a good working relationship. I reminded him that this person was the one who got my husband in trouble.

"He should be facing the most serious charges possible," I insisted.

The chief patiently listened to everything I spewed that day and offered his sympathies to me and what my family was going through. I was waiting to hear some sort of validation from him as to how I thought this kid should be treated. But it never came.

By the end of January 2009, the young man had turned himself into authorities to face several charges including reckless endangering, DUI and aggravated assault.

If only vindication in this sense meant exoneration for Mark. It did not. But something was about to happen to take my attention away from the case.

Between the stress of Mark's case and the anger stemming from it, I was wound tight as a top. I knew it at the time, but I just kept putting one foot in front of the other trying to get the whole nightmare behind us. Until my body told me *enough*.

It was Presidents' Day, so the girls were home from school. I had just finished an hour on the elliptical machine and lifting weights in our basement. Mark and the girls were in the kitchen.

The last thing I remember was walking up the stairs.

I woke up in the emergency room of Moses Taylor Hospital in Scranton.

"Who's the President of the United States?" the doctor asked.

"George Bush," I replied. *Wrong answer.*

Mark's eyes were fixed on mine. He was holding my hand.

"What's going on?" I asked, "Why am I here?"

"When you came upstairs after working out," Mark paused, "You were in a daze. You stared at the calendar and kept asking over and over, *what day is it* and *where are the girls?*"

I do not remember any of that, including the drive to the hospital, but the fog was starting to thin. I suddenly realized that if Mark was at my side, it meant he had left the house with his ankle bracelet.

Mark said he had called the county probation office before he left the house and told the supervisor that there was a family emergency, and he had to get to the hospital immediately. He called his sister to ask her to run to our house to be with the girls.

I was in the hospital for three days of testing. After ruling out a stroke, the doctors believed I suffered a phenomenon known as Transient Global Amnesia (TGA). Patients never lose consciousness and remain attentive, but they lose memory of recent events. The cause is unknown, but some experts believe stressful situations can trigger the condition. Go figure.

My close girlfriends and their husbands came to see me while I was in the hospital, and I was grateful for their kind words and attention. But I could tell by the expressions on their faces they were concerned about my health.

In the weeks that followed, I saw a neurology specialist who ordered a series of tests, including a more detailed MRI to rule out any blockages in the brain. Everything came back fine, although the specialist said I could be more susceptible to developing atherosclerosis or hardening of the arteries in my brain as I got older.

I never regained memory of what happened during those three hours between exercising and waking up in the hospital.

■   ■   ■

As it turned out, my quest to get even with the teen who squealed on Mark came back to haunt me. Months after Mark was released from his house arrest, I was called into the news director's office and shown a cc'd copy of a scathing letter the young man's attorney had sent to the district attorney's office. His attorney accused me of harassing and intimidating his client and his family after the drunk driving crash in many forms, including calling the police chief, contacting the DA's office and generating an "onslaught of unnecessary media coverage to a single DUI accident which did not result in any fatalities." The letter asked the DA's office to look into filing charges against me for harassment and intimidation of a witness.

I sat frozen while my news director waited for me to say something, anything. I could not deny the accusations in the letter. The truth was, I DID contact the police chief and I DID send letters to the DA's office as well as to the boy's family. At that time, it made me feel good to make those calls and send those letters. I wanted to feel the satisfaction of getting back at the person who had wreaked havoc in our lives and caused Mark to lose his job.

But this was a lightbulb moment for me. My all-consuming desire to seek revenge for what this young man had done to Mark evaporated. I realized there was no sound argument to justify my vindictive behavior and poor choices. Seeking revenge had backfired, as it often does.

The precarious situation I found myself in, this time by my own actions, put my job in jeopardy with a defense attorney requesting that the district attorney file charges against me! I promised the news director I would never have contact with anyone associated with this young man's drunk driving case ever again. My boss emphatically told me there would be dire consequences if I broke my promise.

Leaving his office with my tail between my legs, I felt as though I dodged another bullet. But I feared that this latest reprimand, my leave of absence, and the negative publicity tied to Mark's case, were chiseling away at my professional reputation and career at WNEP. Regardless of how popular a TV anchorwoman you are, a television station can, and will, only tolerate so much. And I felt I was at the end of the road.

Luckily, the DA's office never contacted me and did not file charges.

Two years later, this young man pleaded guilty to charges in connection with the drunk driving crash and ultimately served six months in jail. His sentence to time behind bars did not matter. I sincerely regret the well of anger I dipped into to write those letters. I thought revenge would lessen my anger, but instead, it almost caused me more trouble. As the saying goes, *two wrongs don't make a right.* And this was a prime example.

CHAPTER 13

Mark received a severance package when he resigned from NEIU #19. Instead of looking for a new job, he used his one-year probation period to *let things cool down*, as he put it. But at the same time, he seemed to really enjoy being a stay-at-home dad and picking up domestic hobbies along the way. He built a dollhouse for Sarah. He baked and decorated fancy birthday cakes for both of our girls. He cooked and cleaned.

I was grateful I could count on him to manage our home life while I was at work, but I was worried about our financial health. We went from a two-income household to one with increased cost-of-living expenses. How was that going to work? Yet, month after month, Mark still managed to pay the home-equity loan and his half of the mortgage. I had no idea how, but then it dawned on me.

Mark had taken over managing his father's finances because his dad's health was declining. His father had moved from one assisted-living facility to another until a room became available at the Gino Merli Veterans Center in Scranton. My father-in-law passed away there in 2011. But while he was alive, Mark managed his money. After I had this revelation, but before I had a chance to ask where he was getting money, Mark told me he was borrowing money from his father that he planned to pay back when he found work.

. . .

Mark was the one who got in trouble with the law. Mark was the one who pled guilty to furnishing alcohol to minors. But I wore shame and humiliation like a wet, woolen coat that I could not shimmy off and leave in a heap on the floor. I woke up thinking about it. The reality came in and out of my head as I did daily work tasks. I went to sleep thinking about it. And now, I felt like that heavy coat grew large enough to fit my children in it with me.

Mark signed up to be a parent volunteer for a Junior Achievement program call JA BizTown, which teaches 5th and 6th grade students to be business owners. Sarah, now a sixth grader, was excited about her field trip to BizTown. She was even more thrilled that her daddy would be there with her as a volunteer.

But the consequences of Mark's actions were now tangibly affecting the girls.

To be a part of the program Mark had signed a Volunteer Conduct Standards form that included this statement: "had never been charged with a crime of violence or a crime involving a child or a young person." This clearly was not accurate, and it did not escape the eye of the Valley View School District solicitor who sent a letter to Mark's attorney in which he pointed out: "Obviously, the attestation that he has never been charged with a crime involving a young person as of October 14, 2008, is inaccurate."

Mark also never disclosed to the school in writing any facts regarding the charges involving the furnishing of alcohol to minors.

The solicitor called Mark and told him not to participate in the program and Mark agreed not to participate. He also communicated to Mark's attorney that moving forward, he would be prohibited from directly participating as a Valley View coach, advisor, volunteer, etc., in light of his guilty plea. He would still be allowed on Valley View property to see Rachael and Sarah participate in concerts and plays.

I felt sorry for Mark, but I also understood where Valley View was coming from. *If I had been another parent attending that day for JA BizTown—how would I feel seeing Mark there after he had just pleaded guilty to a misdemeanor involving a minor?* I thought.

I left it up to Mark to explain to Sarah why he was not permitted to attend JA BizTown. I figured he *got himself into this mess; he should have to look into her eyes and tell her.* Sarah idolized her father and him being barred from JA BizTown broke her heart. I remember her retreating to her bedroom and crying softly for a while. It was like a dagger to my heart. It certainly would not be the last time Sarah would feel this way.

■   ■   ■

When his probation came to an end, Mark began looking for a job. Because he had been convicted of furnishing alcohol to minors, he lost his state educational license. So that field was no longer an option for him. I think I may have mourned the loss of his license more than he did. He spent all that time, effort and money attaining a Ph.D. in special education, and now it was all for nothing. A friend mentioned to him that Banker's Life and Casualty was looking for agents for their Wilkes-Barre office to sell Medicare supplemental insurance policies. He applied and was hired despite his criminal record.

Mark trained and studied for months before he passed his test and was awarded his license to sell insurance in 2010. He started making an income when he sold Medicare supplemental insurance policies and annuities, and then his salary was based on commission. His income was nothing like what he was making as an educational consultant, but at least it was a job, and we were grateful for it.

Mark's charm, especially with the older people, helped him become fairly successful at Banker's in no time. His commission constantly changed, so I never really knew how much money he was earning, and I did not ask.

As long as he provided me with half the mortgage money every month and fulfilled the payment on the home equity loan, I was okay with whatever he made. What also became an unwritten agreement between the two of us was that Mark would pay for all family vacations and travel.

And we certainly traveled after Mark served his probation. Nothing extravagant, with the exception of our trip to Mexico in October of 2010 that we won at a charity silent auction before Mark got into trouble in 2008. We used the trip to celebrate my 50th birthday. We also continued our traditional Florida summer vacations and our weekend jaunts to the Washington D.C. area to attend football games at Mark's alma mater, the University of Maryland.

We seemed to be back on "perfect-life, happily-ever-after" course after the detour of 2008. Hopefully, it would become a blip that would slowly disappear in the rear-view mirror.

∎   ∎   ∎

The girls were now moving from middle school to high school and were involved in all kinds of activities. Swim team, tennis, band, chorus, clubs, and above all, theater. During fall tryouts in 2011, both girls landed prominent roles in Valley View's musical "Fiddler On The Roof." Sarah got the role of Tzeitel, the eldest daughter, and Rachael played Grandmother Tzeitel who in the musical returns from the grave. They were also growing up at a time when social media was exploding and smartphones were just introduced.

Rachael and Sarah looked at social media as a novel thing but did not jump right into it. I was never a big fan. I shied away from Facebook at work, and I had no interest in it when I got home. I felt it was a time drain, and I certainly did not have extra time in my days to spend on it. I finally joined Facebook after I retired from WNEP in 2016.

For years, the girls and I used flip phones and sent texts by way of typing on those teeny-tiny keyboards. Mark had a flip phone as well, but when smartphones became more popular, allowing internet access to literally be at your fingertips and texting to be much quicker, he traded his flip in for a smartphone. He said he did it because it would be a better tool for work.

At first, I assumed Mark was using texting and social media to stay connected to colleagues and communicate with customers. I saw it as something good, a way for him to build business relationships. And I also assumed it was working since his client list at Banker's kept growing.

But then, his infatuation with the phone increased more and more. I watched Mark get swept up in the social media/tech craze. And eventually, I believe he became addicted to both, and not for purely professionally reasons.

If he was not looking at his laptop, his head was bent over his phone. At dinner, his phone would be on the table. It was becoming more difficult to have a conversation without him glancing down at his phone. It was definitely becoming a distraction everywhere we went. Even in the middle of University of Maryland football games, I would glance over, and see his head bent over his phone, either to post something on Facebook or to send a text. When Rachael and Sarah were swimming in the backyard pool, Mark sat on a lounge chair with his phone in hand.

The girls were beginning to notice, too. I joked with them that it seemed as though their father paid more attention to his phone than he did me.

"Daddy is constantly on his phone," exclaimed the girls. "It is so annoying." They also complained to Mark directly. He would just laugh it off or deny it.

"You're always looking at that phone," I snapped. "I wish you'd pay as much attention to me as you do with that stupid phone of yours."

"No, I'm not," he would say. "I'm paying attention to you."

Mark snickered every time I mentioned it, would then put down his phone and do something else. But a few minutes later, the phone would be back in his hands.

The first thing Mark would do in the morning after he woke up was check his phone. The last thing he did before going to bed was check his phone.

It couldn't all be work-related, I thought. So, out of curiosity, I would occasionally ask him what he was doing on his phone. I sensed he interpreted my inquiry as being nosey and nagging.

"Just checking scores," he would reply. "I'm just checking scores." Taking into account that Mark was an avid sports fan who could recollect statistics like a seasoned ESPN announcer, my interrogation usually went no further. Eventually, I stopped asking.

And I trusted him. I always did. He never gave me a reason not to. In that respect, it never crossed my mind to pick up his cell phone and spy on his texting or calling history. That is something you see a jealous or suspicious wife doing in those Lifetime movies.

Then, something happened that made an uneasy feeling begin to settle in my stomach. When Rachael and Sarah walked into the house one day after school, Mark was so engrossed in his laptop and phone, he failed to look up and say hello, and did not ask how their day was.

"We walked into the house after school, and daddy didn't look at us," Sarah said. Rachael added, "It was like we weren't even there." I remember the sadness and disappointment on their faces when they told me about this later. It was especially difficult for them because they had always been his center of attention.

Mark's phone habit was even caught on camera. The family was posing for photos after the girls performed in "Fiddler on the Roof" in March of 2012. When we looked at all the photos, we noticed that one of them caught Mark looking conspicuously at his cell phone.

It got to the point where I made it mandatory at dinnertime: no more cell phones at the table and any violators would have their cell phones tossed out the front door. Mark laughed at my demand, but he complied with my dinnertime decree. He knew I meant business. The girls did as well, and they made sure their phones did not arrive at the dinner table with them.

.   .   .

In the spring of 2012, Mark decided he no longer was interested in working for Banker's Life and Casualty. He claimed the long hours and traveling to the homes of retirees to sell med-supplemental health insurance policies did not justify the commission. He felt he should have been making a lot more money. He also believed he was under-appreciated by his bosses. He was not the only one. A few other salespeople left at the same time Mark did. His quick move to leave Banker's surprised me in a way because he seemed to be doing so well. I still felt gratitude toward the company and the management team that hired Mark despite his criminal record. But Mark assured me that he already had lined up work with New York Life. He had been working out of the Scranton office, so his commute would be shorter than the drive he had with Banker's.

What I found odd, was that more days than not, Mark appeared to be working from home. The way I said goodbye to him in the morning, sitting on our couch, entrenched with his laptop computer and cell phone, is the way the girls said they found him when they got home from school.

Every time I asked why he was not going into work his answer was always the same.

"I don't need to work from the office all the time," he said. "I can work from home. As long as I can make my appointments from here, everything is fine."

.   .   .

My intense nine-hour work-day schedule had not eased up since I assumed the noon anchor responsibilities back in 2008. But even though I was bone tired when I arrived home most days, I still longed to be intimate with Mark. And yet again, it just was not happening. It was getting to the point where Mark hardly even touched or kissed me. A quick good-morning kiss. A rushed goodbye hug. A good-night peck on the cheek. No handholding while watching TV. When we were out in public, we did not act like a couple. Another wave of rejection was hitting me. What made it worse was listening to my girlfriends talk about how often they still had sex with their husbands.

Had I "let myself go" I might be able to understand Mark's continued lack of interest. But I had not. I took care of my body. Ate well and exercised. I even started getting Botox injections every three months to eliminate brow lines that I thought were noticeable on air. So, why is this man not interested in sex? I just could not understand. My mistake was that I continued to stay silent. I continued to ignore the issue, afraid of what Mark's answer would be.

It was around this time when I noticed that Mark was more and more occupied with his evening trips to the gym. About three or four times a week, as soon as we finished dinner, he would head out and be gone for at least two hours.

He was also striking up more friendships at the gym but not with people his own age. He would come home and ask Rachael, *hey, do you know so-in-so in your class? I was talking to him at the gym tonight.* Soon after, these classmates started showing up at the house, but Mark's explanation was that he offered to pay them to do yard work. It seemed like an innocent enough explanation, and the kids did do work like trimming bushes and cutting grass.

I really did not think much of it until Rachael asked me one day why her father "hung out" with teenagers and not men his own age. She felt embarrassed that these boys she knew from class were at her home because she was not friends with any of them.

When I told Mark about my conversation with Rachael, he had a quick answer, like he always did.

"Some of these guys come from broken homes and are looking for a mentor," he said. "I think I can do a lot of good for them, help them build character."

There are common "tells" when someone isn't being truthful. They might avert their eyes. They might talk faster. They might be fidgety. They might get defensive or angry. Fold their arms. Breathe a little faster. Be vague in their answers. But Mark was super calm, cool, and collected whenever I questioned him about his friendships with these young guys.

So, my suspicions would disappear with his explanations, his demeanor and the trust I always had in him. But as soon as I thought everything appeared normal, or maybe when I convinced myself that everything was normal, there would be another round of odd behavior or bizarre series of events taking place. And yet, I kept believing him.

Around this time, I noticed that Mark was leaving the Bilco doors leading to our basement from our yard open at night. Of course, I asked him why.

"The guys come to see me for help with homework and SAT prep," he said. "And I told them to use that rather than the front door so as not to disturb the girls and you."

Thing is, I also noticed that Mark was coming to bed really late. I would feel him crawl into bed, only to glance at my clock and be surprised that it would read 2 or 3 a.m.

"I was watching TV downstairs in the basement, and I just fell asleep," he said whenever I asked why. I seemed to be asking him why a lot during these years.

In the back of my mind, I could not help but wonder if he was downstairs that late with these teenage boys. Just the thought of that was unnerving and repulsive. It made me shiver. But then again, never did I think Mark would be that stupid to put himself in such a compromising position, especially after what had happened in 2008. I pushed the doubts further back in my mind.

In May, we took another trip to Michigan—this time for my niece Meredith's high-school graduation. Rachael and Sarah were excited to see their cousins. My brother Chris and his wife Nancy, along with the parents of two close classmates of Meredith, threw a beautiful graduation party. My brother expected the extended Burke family to stay through the duration of the get-together, which was scheduled to go well into the evening. But, halfway through, Mark wanted to leave. He insisted on going to the mall because he wanted to buy University of Michigan items for some "friends."

The party was at a country venue a good distance from our hotel and the mall. I wanted to stay, but it made more logistical sense for us to leave as a family, so Mark did not have to come all the way back to get us. Since we had already spent several hours at the party and since it was still going strong with no signs of the crowd thinning, I gave in. Mark dropped the girls and me off at the hotel and headed to the mall alone.

.　.　.

Our early departure from the graduation party did not sit well with the rest of the Burke clan. The next day, we all sensed a cool reception from my brother's family. They were obviously hurt that we left early and interpreted what we did as a snub to Meredith. We left Michigan on rocky terms, and we hardly spoke to one another in the months that followed.

The summer went by quickly and in no time, the girls were headed back to school. Rachael was now a junior and driving. Sarah was now a sophomore.

Because of my work schedule, Mark continued being the parent who chauffeured the girls when he was not lending his car to Rachael. With every trip Mark made to shuttle the girls to after-school activities, events, or part-time jobs, he had the opportunity to be around their friends. And his outgoing personality, quick wit and uncanny knack of relating to younger generations were ever-present. He became familiar with the girls' friends and classmates, knew them by name when I had no idea who they were. The girls thought he was the "cool" dad who knew just-the-right trendy things to say.

But Mark's familiarity with other Valley View kids the girls did not hang out with I believe most likely led to the trouble we encountered that October, and was perhaps the precursor to the huge nightmare that would ensue the following month.

Halloween was still several weeks away, but we woke up numerous times to find our trees and bushes in our front yard draped with toilet paper. It was obvious we were being targeted because no one else had their landscaping dressed in toilet paper. The prank happened at least three times, and each time I was getting more and more annoyed to the point I was contemplating staying up all night to conduct my own surveillance. It was also embarrassing to have toilet paper hanging from our trees in the morning light, not to mention the aggravation of removing all of it, which Mark did. Our neighbors said nothing to us about it. After 2008, most everyone kept their distance from us.

The girls were not able to think of anyone they knew who might be doing this. They seemed worried about who would repeatedly pull off this prank.

I also got angry at Mark who seemed to shrug off what I considered vandalism.

"It's probably some kids who wanted to brag that they t-peed Marisa Burke's house," he said casually. This calmed the girls. But I was more skeptical. His theory did not add up. And when our front door was hit with eggs one night, I exploded.

"What the hell is going on? Why is this only happening to us in the neighborhood and nobody else? It doesn't make sense," I screamed.

So, to appease me, Mark got into his car one evening "to go ask around" in an attempt to catch the culprits. I had no idea where or how he was trying to get this information, but at that point, I figured any effort to find the people responsible would not hurt. After an hour, he returned home knowing no more than when he left.

But something inside me thought there may have been a connection between the toilet paper pranks and the young guys Mark was having over to the house. The same students who asked for help with their schoolwork. The same ones Mark gave money to for doing chores around our house. *If Mark stopped giving them money, was this their retaliation? But why? What was their motivation?* I wondered. Little did I know that just a month later, I would find out.

CHAPTER 14

As much as cell phones have become another appendage for most people, I often see them as extra baggage. And definitely as a distraction. When I anchored the news, I never had mine next to me. I wanted to pay attention to the story and the technique to best deliver that story. I didn't need to be checking email and texts during commercial breaks. News tips and comments about a story just heard on air could wait until the newscast was over. So, when I was in the anchor chair, my cell was on my desk in the newsroom.

I thought my life had changed forever back in 2008 when I got a call about Mark being in legal trouble. But the voicemail left on my phone while I anchored the noon news on November 5, 2012 was going to prove to me that yes, things could get much worse. And that call was the real start of my life changing forever.

It was from my neighbor, Art Saldi. Not only did he live right across the street, but he had built our house. Even after others in the neighborhood kept their distance from us after Mark was charged in 2008, Art and his wife Karen remained our friends. We would often get together between properties just to exchange some kind words or catch up on what was going on in the community. On this day however, his message almost made my heart stop. It definitely brought back an old, familiar knot of panic in my stomach.

Art described seeing all sorts of law enforcement, including the FBI, around my home. All I could think of were those scenes in the movies where the cops have a property surrounded and guns drawn. I held the phone to my ear, frozen in fear, and tried to not let the panic show on my face. The last thing I wanted was to draw any attention from my colleagues. Art added that it looked as though the police were also trying to break down my front door. My heart raced, just like it did in 2008. I felt completely alone in a room buzzing with work-day activity.

I immediately dialed Mark's number. No answer. Then, the horrible flashback to 2008.

This can't be happening again. I thought. *It just can't be.* I was definitely on a slippery slide into shock, fear and terror. No anger... yet.

I dialed Mark's number again, my hands shaking as I was trying to hold the phone. I looked at the clock on the newsroom wall. It was time to head into the afternoon editorial meeting. But how in God's name could I concentrate on any news production at this point? I had to go home, but what would I tell Carl Abraham, the news director? My body was trembling, but I took a deep breath and walked right into his office.

Trying desperately to keep my composure, I said, "I just got a call from a neighbor. There is police activity in my neighborhood. I think I need to go home and find out what's going on. Can someone cover the 6?"

Carl had been around in 2008. I think in that moment we telepathically communicated an entire conversation. I think he was wondering if Mark was in trouble again. I certainly knew from the voicemail that whatever was going on was centered on my home, and I suspected it was about Mark. But I didn't want to say that to Carl or anyone else until I knew exactly what was going on. He reluctantly told me to go home, and always the news hound, reminded me to call the newsroom if the "police activity" warranted a news crew.

Once again, I found myself driving home to Peckville dreading what I was speeding toward. What normally is a 20-minute drive between WNEP-TV and our home seemed more like an hour. I tried calling Mark again, and again, no answer. *Maybe he was actually working from his downtown office today, and he's unable to answer his phone,* I tried telling myself. *Maybe, I'm worrying for nothing.*

I drove into the development and from a distance, it did not look as though there were any police cars at our home. Good sign. Encouraging sign. When I opened the garage door, Mark's car was there. My stomach tightened.

"Hi, honey," he said but did not ask why I was home. I jumped into my interrogation.

"Art left me a voicemail. He said he saw police breaking into our home," I yelled. "Is it true? What happened?"

"Yes, the police were here," Mark replied. "They took electronics again including your iPad and my cell."

That quickly explained why there was no answer when I tried calling Mark earlier.

"Art said he saw cops breaking into our front door?" I exclaimed. "Is this true?"

"I was upstairs in the bathroom when I heard a knock on the front door. Apparently, I didn't get to the door fast enough, so they broke in," Mark said matter-of-factly.

"Broke in?" I screamed furiously. I darted for the front door to see the damage. The frame around the door was split and cracked. The door itself was dented, and the locking mechanisms were broken. "Those bastards!" I shouted.

At the same time, I was frantically looking for answers from Mark. *What the hell were they looking for now?*

"Did they have a search warrant?" I yelled again.

"I think they did," Mark conceded.

"You THINK they did?" I snapped back. "You didn't ask? You didn't call an attorney? They must have had something on you to search the house! What the hell is happening?"

By now I was in hysterics and getting more frustrated by the minute as Mark failed to give me the answers I wanted. Yet again. Just like 2008. He was either withholding some truth or was genuinely baffled as I was. After all, he was not arrested. *If investigators DID have a search warrant,* I thought, *they must have had probable cause to gather even more evidence.* Nothing was making sense to me, and I really had no idea who to call to ask. It was like somebody had hit me really hard over the head with a bat, but I had no clue who was holding the bat.

That afternoon, Mark picked up the girls and took them for a previously-scheduled eye exam. The girls later told me that he had said nothing about what happened at the house until after their appointments. They also told me that "dad seemed very annoyed about what happened but was even more upset that the cops took his phone."

I called Mark's sister and told her what had played out at that day. Without hesitation, she rushed over to our home and offered to take the girls out to dinner so Mark and I could have some time alone to talk. She was visibly upset but was trying to keep a brave face in front of the girls.

For the first time in a long time, Mark could not hide his fear and anxiousness. Even in the aftermath of 2008, I had not ever seen him in such a state. There are moments in a marriage when it feels like all the air is being sucked out of a room. When you just know something is about to be said that will completely change how you think and feel. That night, I was in that room, sealed in with Mark. The air was leaving, and I could not do a damn thing about it.

Yet, I wanted the knowing. I wanted him to open the flood gates. I wanted to know what he knew, what he did not, and most importantly, how he felt at that moment. I wanted total honesty. Just like I had wanted in 2008.

And with a *whoosh* that grew louder and louder, he finally opened up. With tears in his eyes, he admitted that he was using Facebook and texts to communicate with high-school boys, including some in Rachael's class. He confessed that he might be in trouble again because some of those conversations were sexual in nature.

I sat at the kitchen table in disbelief. I was numb, motionless. At first, nothing was coming out of my mouth because I could not believe what I was hearing. But then, I felt compelled to ask the one question that exploded in my head.

"So, you were texting these boys and messaging them, even though you knew it was against the law?" I asked in dismay.

Mark, standing a few feet away from me hesitated, cast his eyes to the floor for a moment, then glanced up, looking straight into my eyes and answered, "yes."

The air was almost completely gone. I felt like I had been gut-punched. Mark had lied to me all along about his behavior, his friendships with these boys, and perhaps the most disturbing thing of all, his own sexuality. *Did I actually marry a pedophile? A homosexual?* Those questions played over and over in my mind.

"Are you gay?" I angrily asked him.

"No," he replied without hesitation.

I didn't believe him. Again, I thought he was lying to protect his wholesome, good-guy image. And then my thoughts started tumbling through my mind like a waterfall – when Mark took me to a bed and breakfast for our tenth anniversary and what I thought it would be a romantic get-away turned into a night without sex… to 2008 when Mark blamed that 17-year-old for getting him in trouble and made it seem as though he was being targeted by the district attorney's office because we were both high-profile people… to my rage at Gene Talerico…to my wanting revenge against the 17-year-old.

How wrong I had been about it all.

How naïve I had been.

The Lackawanna County detectives, investigators and Gene Talerico were right all along; their case was not an exaggeration. My husband was preying on young guys, many underage, and God only knows what his ulterior motive was. It was both sickening and disgusting to think I was married to this individual, that I slept with him, made a life with him, provided for him, trusted him.

And yet, as devastated and heartbroken as I was, this was the moment of my epiphany. I woke up in a second. This person was clearly not the man I married. So many questions swirled, but I was clear on one thing. I needed to drastically course correct. I would not repeat 2008. I could not. I could no longer support and defend this man who I tirelessly devoted my life to for nearly 20 years. I now saw the man I was honored to call my husband and proud to say the father of my children as a con man who betrayed his family. I had to make a change – for my daughters and me.

I looked at Mark.

"This time, you're on your own," I said, as I did the washing-of-the-hands gesture people make when they absolve themselves from wrongdoing.

I was standing under a waterfall of relief. I could breathe again. Mark bowed his head and started to cry. An emotion I had not seen in him for a long, long time.

CHAPTER 15

After a sleepless night of tossing and turning fueled by wondering and worrying about the next ax about to fall, I had no choice but to get up, get dressed and get to work because it was Election Day. Cardinal rule in journalism: you never skip Election Day. But the day after our house was once again raided, it took every bit of energy, strength, and professionalism for me to go on the air like nothing was wrong. That familiar excruciating knot of fear in my stomach refused to loosen, and I had visions of getting yet another phone call about Mark.

Election Day came and went. No phone call. I actually had a glimmer of optimism that perhaps the second search and seizure at our home was all for naught. Maybe investigators thought they would find something on Mark's phone or laptop, but found nothing. That hope quickly vanished the next day.

November 7, 2012 started out like any other normal day. Mark took the girls to school, returned home and appeared to be doing office work, minus of course, his laptop and phone. Mark and I had spoken very little since the day of the search. What few words we did say were very matter of fact, cold, and forced. I was happy leaving the tension-filled house to head to work.

A few hours later, it all came crashing down. Around mid-morning, I was at my cubicle writing scripts for the noon newscast when Carl called me into his office.

"Marisa, we just got word that the DA's office is arresting Mark," he said. "You better go home. We'll cover for you here."

I stared at my boss for a few moments. My reporter's instinct wanted desperately to ask how he found out that they were going to arrest Mark. *Who contacted WNEP? Why didn't they let me know first?* But nothing came out of my mouth. It was like having a horrible nightmare but not being able to scream out loud.

I was looking for some, any, reassurance that my job would not be in jeopardy despite what was facing Mark this time. That reassurance never came. Carl really did not know what else to say and neither did I, so I left his office, walked over to my desk, packed my things and left, wondering if I would ever return. The station tolerated the bad publicity in 2008. Would they do the same for another scandal just four years later? *No way,* I thought. I was convinced that my long, prosperous career as a broadcast journalist at WNEP-TV was finished.

Unlike four years ago, I immediately channeled my shock and anguish into anger. Not at law enforcement. Not at the DA's office. But toward Mark.

At this point, I had no idea exactly what kind of trouble he was in, but I assumed it had to do with the high schoolers who were showing up at our house. I wanted answers that could only come from speaking with Mark or police officers. But my priority as I left work that morning was getting my girls from school before the news broke to the public.

I knew the people in the front office of Valley View High School. They were always cordial and helpful anytime I had to go to the school. I told them we had a family emergency and that I needed to take the girls home.

They immediately asked, "Is everything all right?"

"I don't know yet," I replied, knowing full-well that if they were to go online in a few short hours, they would know exactly what was developing.

Both girls showed up at the office around the same time.

"Hey there, you two," I said in a light voice that probably sounded heavily forced. "Something came up, and I need to take you out of school for the rest of the day."

Rachael and Sarah looked worried and panicked. It was heartbreaking. I felt the tears rising, but I tried my best not to break down in the office, so I hurried them out to the car. Once we were all in the car, I told them that their father had been arrested again. They wanted to know what for, but I could not give them an answer because I did not know.

"What happened this time, Mom?" Rachael asked nervously in the front seat.

"Does it have something to do with those boys in Rachael's class?" asked Sarah sitting behind us. "Is this going to be on the news again?"

"I really don't know until I talk with your father," I answered.

"So, you're not going back to work today?" Sarah asked again.

"No, they let me go home and be with you two," I said.

I knew Mark's arrest was trickling to news outlets, and it would just be a matter of time before news crews showed up at our house again. So instead of going there, we went to Mark's sister's house in Scranton, thinking that it would be a shelter. I needed to protect the girls as best I could. The hours leading into the evening were spent consoling Rachael and Sarah who worried what their friends and classmates would say about their father's arrest.

I remember pacing back and forth, with a glass of wine in my hand, trying to calm down, and waiting for any word from Mark or perhaps an attorney he had contacted about arranging bail. Having been an employee in Scranton's Public Works Department, Mark's sister knew people in city government and law enforcement. She was on the phone constantly that afternoon. Bit by bit, she was starting to gather information, and it was not good. At the same time, the news was hitting online. Kim, her partner, the girls and I were all reading our phones in disbelief. And by the afternoon newscasts, Mark's arrest was the lead story. On Newswatch 16 at 4 p.m.:

"We are going to begin today with a story that is very difficult for us to report, but in fairness, we must. We learned this afternoon that Mark Kandel of Peckville, the husband of Newswatch 16s Marisa Burke, was arrested on charges of sex abuse with a minor. Kandel was brought to the Lackawanna County Courthouse this afternoon to face the charges filed by the county detectives. He is charged with criminal solicitation to create child pornography."

I lacked the courage to turn on the TV, but Mark's sister was watching on her phone and reporting it to me. I was knocked off my feet by "sex abuse, minor, criminal solicitation and child pornography." These are serious crimes against children—cases that made me sick every time I had to report accusations of this kind on the news. But now, the accusations were lodged against my husband! And this was much worse than the charges in 2008. It felt like I was standing on the beach just as a hurricane made landfall.

That feeling of just getting in the car and driving away with the girls I first had back in 2008 kept washing over me like unending waves. I did not want to feel that humiliation and embarrassment again. But deep down, I knew there was no curling up and hiding from it.

I understood why the news outlets including Newswatch 16 had to mention me. They would have been remiss had they not mentioned my name. But it was still mortifying to see and hear my name broadcast all over the news again and published online. The shame was nauseating.

After the 4 o'clock news where they briefly announced Mark's arrest and said there 'would be much more extensive coverage coming up at 5 and 6,' I decided that I could not stomach to watch/read/listen anymore. I disconnected from the news, Mark, the situation. *Where do I go from here?* I kept wondering. Kim kept the television off so as not to upset the girls. But she kept track of the coverage on her computer and on her phone.

Hours filled with anxiety passed from late afternoon to evening. The girls and I were drained. I wanted to get us home and into bed. If any news crews had gone live in front of our house for the early newscasts, I figured they had packed up and left by now. Sure enough, when I pulled into Blythe Drive, the neighborhood was eerily quiet.

Late that night, after Mark posted 10% cash of a $20,000 bail, he was released from jail but instead of coming home he went to his sister's house. I never asked why because I really did not care. I presumed he did not have the guts to confront me about what he was being accused of this time. That was fine with me. My anger was at an all-time high. I do not think I could have spoken to him even if I had wanted to. And there was something so dirty about all this. I was so disgusted and did not want to be around that or him.

My phone rang as I was getting myself ready for bed that night. It was my friend Jackie. Unlike four years ago when all I wanted was to go into seclusion, I was hoping that someone, anyone, would reach out to me to see how I was doing. All my close friends must have watched the news or seen something about Mark online. Leave it to Jackie to be the first one to call.

"How are you, my friend?" she asked as soon as I answered the phone. "What the hell has happened this time?"

I didn't know where to begin to tell her the nightmare that was starting up all over again. I started crying. We were probably on the phone for over an hour as I described what lead to Mark's arrest and what authorities were accusing him of this time. I told her that this time, Mark was on his own. The energy to stick up for him was gone, to defend him as I did in 2008.

"Fool me once, shame on you. Fool me twice, shame on me," I said to Jackie. She agreed.

"Hang in there, my friend," she said as our conversation was coming to a close. "I will be here for you every step of the way."

Obviously, I was given some time off from work after Mark's arrest hit the news. As much as I was worried whether I would have a job to return to, my biggest concern was how Mark's criminal trouble and the continuous news coverage were going to affect the girls. That night I called their guidance counselor to see if I could meet the next morning with the high school administration. High schoolers can be heartless and all I could picture was Rachael and Sarah being ridiculed at school because of their father. I desperately wanted some sort of assurance this would not happen or at least, measures would be taken to try to prevent the girls being made fun of in any way.

I let the girls decide about school the next day. Rachael stayed home. Many of the students Mark talked to were in her journalism class, and she was afraid classmates would ridicule her. Mark had not befriended anyone in Sarah's class, so she was in a different position than Rachael, and she insisted on going to class.

My primary focus was making sure the girls were okay both physically and emotionally. We refused to watch any TV news or read anything online that morning. The girls' guidance counselor arranged for a morning meeting at school that included the principal and vice principal. Since Sarah was at school, she was also included in the meeting.

The principal, Peter Chapla, was a former Marine. He never put up with nonsense and was known for being a disciplinarian at Valley View. All three administrators were so sympathetic, understanding and compassionate, and Chapla reassured us that the school would not tolerate any ridicule from classmates, whatsoever. He promised that if there were any such behavior by any student, parents would be notified immediately, and the student would be sent home. I started crying uncontrollably. I was grateful for the administrators' compassion and professionalism. But I was also crying because I knew how cruel, intentionally or not, kids can be. It would break my heart if I found out that anybody was making fun of my precious girls.

That afternoon when Sarah returned home from school, I was relieved to hear her day was nothing out of the ordinary. If classmates talked about her father, she said, the conversations must have been done behind her back because no one said anything directly to her.

Mark waited until that evening to show up at the house, and he had his new attorney in tow. My impression was that Mark seemed overly confident and nonchalant even though he was facing serious charges. He was acting as if authorities got it wrong again and that he was going to beat these new allegations.

Outside of the girls asking him if he was okay, we barely spoke to him. What we found odd was that he really gave no indication he wanted to talk with us. We were expecting him to offer some sort of explanation, or to at least say, "I'm sorry." But it never happened. Instead, he casually escorted his attorney into our formal living room to review the arrest papers and to presumably begin drafting a defense.

Rather than using the same attorney he hired in 2008, Mark chose a new one based on a recommendation of a friend who described him as a pitbull and thought he would be appropriate to handle Mark's case. I wondered if he was in well over his head tackling this high-profile criminal case. Even though Mark and I were hardly speaking to each other, Mark wanted to give the impression that we were unified and that I was still supportive of him. After several minutes alone with his attorney, Mark called me into the living room.

"Honey, I wanted you to meet Frank. He's agreed to represent me. He doesn't think the county has much of a case against me."

I had no reaction. I said nothing. Then Mark's new attorney chimed in.

"There are some damaging and incriminating aspects in this affidavit," he said with an air of confidence, "but I really think their evidence isn't all that strong."

His remarks were ominous, yet ambiguous. Again, I did not react. Instead, I asked to see the affidavit of probable cause, and after reading it, I was more convinced than ever that Mark was in serious trouble.

AFFIDAVIT OF PROBABLE CAUSE

BACKROUND OF INVESTIGATION

On May 28th, 2008 Affiant Kolcharno arrested Mark Kandel, age 48 of 5 Blythe Drive Peckville, for Selling or Furnishing Liquor or Malt or Brewed Beverages to Minors. Prior to his arrest, Kandel was employed as a PH.D level curriculum specialist at the Northeast Educational Intermediate Unit (NEIU) #19 in Archbald, PA. The NEIU coordinates the educational needs for special needs children throughout Northeastern Pennsylvania. Affiant Kolcharno, a class "A" wiretap certified officer, Certification number A-3322 conducted a consensual intercept under intercept number 57 C-08-062. In this investigation, Kolcharno recorded text message and phone conversation initiated by KANDEL to a juvenile's cell phone. The call was initiated by KANDEL to the juvenile while both were "texting".

During the intercepted communication, KANDEL verified that he had a party at his residence and agreed to e-mail photographs he had taken at the party. He agreed to send the pictures to the juvenile's iPhone. This detective intercepted the images sent to the juvenile's cell phone which depicted youths drinking alcohol at the KANDEL residence. Bottles of beer, red party cups of beer and persons drinking from shot glasses were depicted in the photographs. KANDEL was also depicted with the juvenile in a photograph from that evening. This activity demonstrated that KANDEL is comfortable in sending images, including images which are potentially incriminating. Kandel was arrested and plead guilty to Furnishing alcohol to Minors in the Lackawanna County Court of Common Pleas.

Since this prior arrest, your affiants have received multiple complaints regarding Mark Kandel having inappropriate online relationships and physical contact with minors. Said complaints were investigated, however, criminal charges were not able to be established. The common plan, scheme or design of Kandel's contact included texts and conversation telling teenaged boys they would look sexually attractive if they wore Calvin Klein boxer briefs. Kandel offered and took multiple males on shopping excursions where he bought expensive designer clothing, including boxer brief underwear and compression shorts. Kandel has also taken multiple teenaged males to lunch at Café Soriano and Coccetti's located in Peckville, PA. Kandel was observed by Detective Michelle Mancuso at approximately Christmas of 2011, purchasing sneakers for two males at Dick's Sporting Goods in Dickson City, PA. Affiant Kolcharno was summoned by WalMart loss prevention in August of 2012. KANDEL was observed with a teenaged boy and purchased him $59.00 worth of boxer briefs and compression shorts. Your affiants have received information in that Kandel believes that he is a form of a life-coach, for teenage boys.

Kandel was also engaged in texting males and meeting or waiting for them at their workplaces throughout Lackawanna County.

On October 12, 2011 Affiant LERI and Detective Mancuso received information that Kandel had been contacting a 16 year old male, via text message and Facebook messages. Utilizing Facebook account: HYPERLINK http://www.facebook.com/mark.kandel.16

www.facebook.com/mark.kandel16

The juvenile male stated that Kandel had requested his friendship on Facebook and began messaging him through Facebook messenger in late summer of 2011 through the Fall. The juvenile male stated that he had become "freaked out," with the messages that Kandel had been sending him, and he stopped responding. He stated that Kandel had been continually asking him about the "speedo" swimwear he utilized during swim season. He further stated that Kandel began calling him "speedo boy," and "fuzz stud."

The juvenile's parents then granted Detective Leri consent to assume the online identity of the 16 year old juvenile male. Detective Leri then began an undercover operation as a 16 y.o. male utilizing text messaging to converse with Kandel at Verizon cellular number (570) 466-0582, identified as the cellular number belonging to Kandel. Det. MANCUSO, a certified class "A" wiretap officer, would be intercepting the communications.

In October 2011, LERI, as an undercover 16 y.o. male, began conversing via text messages with Kandel. Throughout the conversation, Kandel referred to the UC as "speedo boy," and would continually question the UC on what types of underwear he wears and if he likes wearing speedos. Kandel stated that he like the "playfulness" of the UC. At the end of the conversation Kandel stated, "I know u are a good Christian Kid and wouldn't be trying to harm me or set me up."

Although no criminal charges were warranted based on the UC operation, Detectives established a pattern of communication used by Kandel.

SPECIFIC PROBABLE CAUSE

On 11/01/2012 Your affiants were contacted by email from a 17 year old juvenile male, through the Lackawanna County District Attorney's Office tip-line. The juvenile victim stated that he had been involved in text message communications with a Mark Kandel, "doc." He stated that the messages were very perverted and he continued to go along with the messages because he was afraid of stopping. The juvenile male also furnished investigators with a screen shot of text messages and a cellular device image, which he described was a picture sent to him, from Kandel. This picture appeared to be Kandel wearing compression underwear, with a bulge in the crotch area.

On 11/02/2012, your affiants made contact with the juvenile male and his family. The juvenile male met with detectives at Blakely Police Department on 11/02/2012 at approximately 2000 hours. In an interview with detectives, the juvenile male stated that in early October 2012, he had met Kandel, through his friends. He stated that his friends had told him that Kandel would help them with their school work. During the meeting, Kandel gave the juvenile victim his business card, and circled his cellular number as "570 466 0582" and email address of HYPERLINK mailto:mwkandel@aol.com. mwkandel@aol.com.

The juvenile male stated he had communicated with Kandel via email, asking Kandel for help with a college entrance essay. He further stated that during the email communications, Kandel had again given him his cellular number and told him to text message him, if he wanted to talk.

The juvenile male stated that his text message conversation with Kandel, first appeared harmless in nature, but quickly escalated to sexual content. He stated that he became nervous with the text messages, and continued to go along with Kandel. The juvenile male victim stated that at one point he was going to provide Kandel with nude pictures of himself, in exchange for money or other favors. He also stated that Kandel had wanted to meet him, multiple times, for what he believed to be sexual encounters. He denied any sexual relations with Kandel. The juvenile male stated that he had not deleted any of the text messages with Kandel, against the advice of Kandel, who insisted he delete everything.

LERI performed a forensic extraction of the juvenile male's cellular device and noted multiple text message communications between the victim and

Kandel, with a cellular device number of 570.466.0582, as seen in prior investigations.

LERI and KOLCHARNO began examination of the text communications between the juvenile victim and Kandel. Detectives noted approximately 900 messages throughout the month of October 2012.

Detectives noted that the text communication began with discussion of Kandel's help with the juvenile male's essay. The conversations quickly progressed into sexual connotations including asking what type of underwear the juvenile male was wearing, penis size and grooming of the pubic area. In the conversations, Kandel asks "boxers or briefs?," "Yukaonly small guys wear boxers;),""u shave or trim?." Kandel refers to the juvenile male as "boxer boy," and stated "always listen to me boxer boy..u need briefs or tighties;),"id love to see u in tighties..Iwear them with dress pant." As conversation progresses, Kandel refers to the juvenile male's grooming in that, "I say shave your boysashave a patch above your monsterathen crop it low..if ya have a hairy butt shave it;).

As the conversations with the juvenile male progressed, Kandel asked when the juvenile male would be turning 18 years old. Kandel used "toy" names for the juvenile male, including "boddy, boxer boy, stud, turtleballs, bubblebutt, sparky, cornhole, good boy, turtle dick, ballsack, hairnuts, tightass and Mr. CD.

Throughout this time frame, Kandel questions the juvenile male on his penis size, asking "U thick? Or average?," and at one point asking the juvenile male if his penis was erect and to measure it. He then stated that he would "double check for ya when ya come over," and "U think I'm kiddinalmao." He continually questioned the juvenile male, asking if he was "spankin it'," meaning masturbating.

At multiple points during the month of October, Kandel and the juvenile male discussed transferring sexual pictures of the juvenile male to Kandel on CD or memory card. In referring to the transfer of pictures, Kandel stated "U are really into this..lol u are one smart cookie;)." This conversation also included the juvenile male being compensated for the pictures. When the juvenile male asked if he could send the pictures via cellular device, Kandel responded "No..nothing via phone..lol," and "Will it be your junk? Lmao." Kandel then referred to the juvenile male as "Mr. CD."

Text message content also revealed multiple instances of Kandel wanting to meet with the juvenile male, including visits to his work place and at his school. In another instance, Kandel discussed meeting with the juvenile male for "front and back massages."

On Monday November 5, 2012, your affiants obtained a search warrant for Kandel's residence at 5 Blythe Drive, Peckville, PA, signed by Lackawanna County Court of Common Pleas.

Judge Barrasse. Detectives with the Lackawanna County District Attorney's Office, Pennsylvania State Police Computer Crime Task Force, Blakely Police Department and FBI executed a search warrant on the resident. Multiple computer related items including Kandel's cellular device with cellular number 570 466 0582, were seized.

Kandel was mirandized and interviewed by investigators. During the course of the interview, Kandel stated that the Verizon cellular number 570 466 0582 was his and furthermore that he does engage in sexual communications with teenage boys, whom are under the age of 18 through his cell phone and Facebook account. Kandel stated that he had very good relationships with teenage boys, including those from troubled homes, and considers himself a mentor.

He stated that when the parents of these boys do not show an interest in their lives, he is the one who will go to their games and help them financially.

Kandel described the sexual messages to underage boys as "joking," but later stated that these sexual messages do have some truth. Kandel was asked if he could describe his state of mind during these conversations, as the conversations quickly go from harmless to sexual. Kandel acknowledged that he becomes overwhelmed with sexual feelings.

I felt physically sick after reading the affidavit. *"Kandel acknowledged that he becomes overwhelmed with sexual feelings."* I kept myself from even looking at Mark. My blood was near boiling. I was disgusted to know that I slept with this monster and that he was still sharing our bed! How could this man, the father of my children, evolve into someone so perverted?

Everything was becoming so clear.

No wonder Mark never had any extra money given what he was spending on taking these boys out, and buying them clothes and gifts, including new cell phones. The University of Michigan items he insisted on buying back in May? They had to be for those boys! No wonder he left me to assume financial responsibility for most of our family and household expenses. No wonder he was constantly looking at his phone. And no wonder he did not want sex with me anymore.

The court papers established a pattern of immoral behavior that dated back to 2008 when he furnished alcohol to minors. Four years ago, Mark dismissed his text message about grooming private parts as "locker room humor." It was now obvious that Mark exploited his education and status to impress and deceive the young men into thinking that he was a mentor when, in reality, he was a predator. Unfortunately, it took me this long to realize that Mark's constant attention to his cell phone was not "just checking scores," but instead was his tool to entice and communicate with underage boys.

What was particularly glaring from the Lackawanna County arrest papers was the number of texts between Mark and his juvenile victims. Our phone plan included unlimited data, so for the most part, the monthly Verizon bill was the same amount. I really never felt the need to scour through the bills carefully to access details about usage. After reading the affidavit against Mark, though, I had to see for myself.

The first thing I did the next day was hunt down household bills. The girls had gone back to school, but I was home since WNEP gave me a few days off after Mark's arrest. It took me a bit of time to rummage through a stack of paperwork to find our Verizon bills. Now I wish I had looked at the usage details more closely each month. The proof was spelled out in black and white. The shocking truth. The evidence that backed up what was in the affidavit, only worse.

Mark had sent more than 17,000 text messages in one month! The affidavit of probable cause mentioned 900 text messages. But those were the messages between Mark and one boy. Who were sent the other text messages and how many more? *How in the hell can anybody send tens of thousands of texts a month?* I asked myself. I called Mark upstairs to the bedroom.

"I just looked at some recent Verizon bills, including this one from October," I screamed as I waved the bill in the air. "Can you explain your 17,000 text messages in one month?"

"That's got to be a mistake," Mark snapped. "It has to be a mistake." But he never asked to look at the bill.

"You mean to tell me that the Verizon phone company made an error with these bills when it came to your text messages?" I asked sarcastically. "You really expect me to believe that shit?"

"Believe what you want," Mark exclaimed, "but I know I wasn't texting that often." And with that, he walked out of the room.

I just could not wrap my head around the denial Mark was in. How much he was focusing on everyone else being wrong. How much he thought he was right. How much he believed his own stories.

Now I was not only living with a pervert, I was living with a liar and a narcissist. A pathological liar. I could not stand the fact that he was still in our home and appearing as though the latest charges against him were no big deal. His nonchalant attitude and manner infuriated me. Something had to be done. And it started with me kicking him out of our bed.

CHAPTER 16

The week Mark was arrested, my news director Carl called me and suggested a short leave. No being on air in the public spotlight. No work at all. He said we would touch base in a few days when things settled down.

I seriously thought the second criminal case against Mark would be the end of my career at the station, and I was already contemplating how I would support my girls and myself if I suddenly lost my job. On top of that, I never disclosed to management what the "police activity" was all about at our home the day before election day. But the raid was revealed in Mark's arrest papers, which is public record. Even so, my supervisors never came down on me for that. I presume it was because they felt so sorry for me.

That weekend, I packed up the girls and retreated to my mother's house. My girls loved spending time at their nana's house because they got to sleep in the same room upstairs. My old bedroom was right across the hall. I could not bear to be anywhere around the Scranton area. I could only imagine what people were saying behind my back this time. *See, you should have left the fucking idiot after the first time he got into trouble,* echoed through my brain.

My mother did the best she could to get my mind off the mess I was in, but it was difficult not to cry in front of her. "I don't know what I'm going to do," I kept saying to her repeatedly. "How could he do this to his family. How could he do this to me?"

That Friday night I must have collapsed from all the stress and strain. I do not even remember falling asleep. The next morning, we were having breakfast when out of the corner of my eye, I saw a figure walking quickly up the driveway of my mother's house. The way my mother had her curtains arranged blocked most of the view, but I knew somebody was approaching the house. Suddenly, the back door swung open. It was my older brother Chris and his wife Nancy from Michigan! They had left Ann Arbor the day before and spent the night somewhere in western Pennsylvania before getting up early to get to our mom's house in Riverside. They traveled 500 miles (one way) just because they needed to see, in person, how the girls and I were doing. My mom must have tipped them off earlier in the week that I was coming home after Mark's arrest. We all hugged and cried and for the first few moments after their arrival none of us really knew what to say to one another. But I felt the compassion and concern of a big brother for his little sister. And this, despite the falling out we had after Meredith's graduation. I will never forget that they drove from Michigan to Pennsylvania and then back to Michigan in the span of three days just to check in on Rachael, Sarah and me. That is love. That is family.

■　　■　　■

That Sunday evening after I returned from my mother's house, Carl called me and asked me to come back to work on Monday.

"Are you sure you want me back?" I asked with apprehension.

He reminded me that we were in the midst of the November ratings period, and they did not want me or any other anchor off the air. Carl suggested that returning to work might also be a welcome distraction from all the turmoil connected with Mark and a way to reinforce to our viewers that I had nothing to do with Mark's crimes. Therefore, there was no need for me to stay out of the anchor chair and go into hiding.

After I talked with Carl, I spent hours catching up on all sorts of chores— washing clothes, cleaning up the kitchen, vacuuming carpets. I was trying to keep my mind occupied while trying to figure out how to move my life forward and out of this mess. As I was putting away clothes and picking out an outfit for the next day, I sat down to play with my dog Molly for a few minutes. I glanced at my left hand. At that moment, my wedding band and engagement ring suddenly symbolized something grotesque. It was my bond to Mark, and I now wanted that bond broken. I wanted to be disconnected from him. And removing my rings would be the first step.

Even so, it felt odd to slide my engagement ring and then my wedding ring off my finger where they had been since my wedding day in 1994, but I knew in my heart it was time. I knew it was the right thing to do. Taking them off was also the first time the thought crossed my mind that my marriage might end.

Growing up, I dreamed of a happy marriage. Children to love. A home in which to raise them. And while there had been some potholes, I thought we were cruising on that American-dream road. But now, I felt like I had reached a roadblock where the road had been completely washed out on the other side. I felt like I was married to a stranger, a man accused of so many ugly and disgusting crimes against children.

Children! You can't get much worse than that, I thought over and over again shaking my head like I could rid my mind of those images, and if I did, they would suddenly disappear. This would all suddenly be just a bad, bad nightmare.

My girls noticed immediately that my rings were missing from my left hand, especially Rachael who never missed a beat whenever something looked different.

"Mom, are you keeping your rings off just for now because you're mad at daddy?" asked Rachael. "Or do you think you'll eventually wear them again?"

"I'm not sure what the heck I'm doing right now or where my mind is," I answered.

Rachael looked at me with such sadness in her eyes. But she kept quiet. She was old enough to know this was a very serious situation and things might not ever be the same.

When I went back on the air that Monday, I felt as though all 631,000 viewers in northeastern and central Pennsylvania were staring right at me waiting to see if I would say anything about Mark, what my expression would be, my demeanor. A tremendous amount of self-control helped me anchor the news like I would on a normal day, and I was drained at the end of my shift. But I was determined to anchor the news minus my rings. I assumed our most loyal and observant viewers, some who asked if I was pregnant before even showing on air, would notice. And I hoped they did. I hoped it sent a message about how I felt about Mark and that this time, I was not on his side.

•　　■　　■

Mark lived in limbo after his arrest. New York Life had to let him go. So, he was out of a job – again. And once again, he became a stay-at-home dad. Yet it appeared being unemployed did not bother him. His biggest frustration seemed that he was without his cell phone, which was confiscated during the raid of our home, so he bought a track phone. At least he could use it to coordinate driving the girls to after-school activities, sporting events, appointments, and to their jobs.

When my brothers and I were in high school, our dad lost his job at the bank. At the time, we did not fully understand what had happened. He simply came home one day and announced he had been let go. No more job. No more salary. We were now a household of one income. Our mom probably never wanted to share the whole story with us. But later on, we learned the bank board felt my father was taking too many risks when it came to approving mortgages for first-time home buyers.

What our mom did share was her devastation. She had grown to love the notoriety and prestige that came with being married to a bank executive. On top of that, my father's job loss happened at the worst time. The expense of college times three was at our doorstep. But to my mother's credit, she gathered her courage and determination and let go of the devastation and despair. Along with her teaching job, she began moonlighting as a hostess at the restaurant where my older brother was working as a cook, and I as a waitress. My younger brother soon joined us, so for a while we felt like the Burkes were running the joint.

My father eventually found work, first for a restaurant supply company and then a variety store in Danville. But the jobs paid nowhere near what he was making as a bank manager. Somehow, my parents put us all through college without taking out any school loans. Today, that is nearly impossible, unless you are super wealthy. But we persevered as a family, and my father's ordeal made us stronger and more humble. We also learned the hard lesson that life can throw you a curveball at a moment's notice.

While Mark had lost his NEIU job in 2008, this job loss felt different. More ominous. Our girls were a couple of years away from college. And now, we were living on just my income. It seemed time to summon that determination and courage I saw my mom use all those years ago.

Mark was spending quite a bit of time at his attorney's office; I assumed contemplating strategy for his case and upcoming preliminary hearing, whenever that was going to be. I never asked what the meetings were about and what was discussed because I really did not care. Mark and I spoke very little during this time. All I was concerned about was protecting my girls and trying to keep their lives as normal as possible considering the mess their father had dragged us all into.

Not too long after I returned to work, I made another important decision to prove that I was separating myself from Mark. On a cold, November afternoon, Mark and the girls were snuggled up on the sectional downstairs in our basement watching television. He seemed as though he did not have a care in the world, like it was just an ordinary day of hanging out in the basement with the girls. The aggravation I felt that minute made what I was about to say easy. I made my way downstairs.

"I have something to announce," I said as I stared at all three who seemed a bit irritated that I interrupted whatever they were watching. I turned off the television and then looked directly at Mark.

"Considering the charges against you, I have decided that you are no longer permitted to live here as your case goes through the court system," I said calmly standing there in front of him and the girls. "You can go live with either your sister in Scranton or your brother in New Jersey. I want you out as soon as you're ready. You can go pack your things, and I will give you time alone to say goodbye to the girls. But you have to go."

For a few moments, Mark was silent then said, "I can understand why you are doing this. And if this is what you want, I'll go." His eyes started filling with tears, and he reached out to hug the girls. They also started crying.

I felt nothing. I had no pity for him whatsoever. All emotion was gone. I had already kicked him out of my bed. He had been sleeping in the guest room.

When I made that decision, I think I knew in the back of my mind that this would be the next step. It felt right.

"You need to pack and leave immediately, Mark," I said.

I turned around, went upstairs and closed the basement door to give him privacy while saying goodbye to the girls. Being separated from them would be most excruciating for him, but I did not care. It was about time he started feeling the underlying pain I had endured since 2008 and was suffering all over again with another criminal case against him, and this one much worse. I hoped he was being hit with wave after wave of remorse. I never saw that in 2008, and I certainly was not seeing any regret now. As heartbreaking as it was listening to the girls cry, I knew it was one of the best decisions I made during this ordeal.

Mark came upstairs with the girls. He headed directly for our bedroom. The girls went to their rooms, shut their doors, and continued to sob. It was hard, but I gave them space.

Mark left with very few belongings, a few personal hygiene items and some clothes. Perhaps this was done in spite, to show me that he thought his eviction would only be temporary. It did not matter. I felt relieved when his car pulled out of the driveway. I had no idea where he was going, nor did I care.

Eventually Mark landed at his brother's house in New Jersey. When I asked his sister why she did not allow him to stay with her, she said that her partner did not want him there because of the criminal case against him and all the attention it was getting. Not surprising given the charges. It was the same reason I demanded that he leave our house.

He had no income, no job, just the car that I bought for him. And very soon, he would not have that either.

■   ■   ■

During those remaining weeks in November, Mark would drop by the house every so often and unannounced, to retrieve fresh clothes, check his mail and meet with his attorney. When his visits overlapped times that I was also home, we rarely spoke except to argue about money. I insisted that he was still responsible for half the mortgage, and he promised he would give me the money. At this point I really did not care how he scraped up the money, but I stressed that I still needed to keep the household going for the sake of the girls whether he was there or not. I could not imagine making the girls move from the home they loved, and the only one they remembered, because of financial difficulties. I simply could not let that happen.

When Mark was in town on the weekends, I did allow him to spend alone time with Rachael and Sarah. He usually picked them up and took them out somewhere for a few hours, almost like what divorced fathers do when they have visitation rights. One weekend however, Mark showed up with a car for Rachael, and it was not some beat-up jalopy.

He called us out to the driveway. There sat a black 2004 Audi A4. It belonged to his friend at Banker's who connected him to his new attorney. His friend did not want the car any longer, so he offered it to Mark as long as Mark would pay off what was left on the car loan.

Before I even had a chance to ask how in the hell we were going to afford payments on a third vehicle, Mark said, "The payments are only $250 a month. And I'll cover it. At least Rachael will have a set of wheels to get her and her sister to and from school. And she can get to her job on her own."

Rachael was elated and repeatedly thanked her father for the car. I was happy for her, but I said nothing to Mark, turned around and went back into the house. I never knew how handy that car would be until a few weeks later.

■   ■   ■

As much as the girls wanted a "normal" Thanksgiving that year with all of us together, I was adamant that Mark not be included in our family holiday. The girls knew how angry I was and they understood my decision. I took them to my mother's house, and the four of us had a quiet, pleasant Thanksgiving dinner.

After Thanksgiving, the girls and I discussed the possibility of allowing Mark to come for Christmas.

"We don't see any harm in it," they said. "It would be just for a little while."

I could see in their faces how much they wanted their father to be included in the holiday. And in that moment, I actually had an ounce of pity for him. I knew how heartbroken Mark would be if he could not spend at least some of the Christmas holiday with his girls. Reluctantly, I agreed that he could spend a few days at home, and it made the girls very happy.

During one of his "drop-ins" that month, I explained that it had cost $300 to repair the damage to the front door when authorities raided our home. He knew how angry I was considering this was money coming out of MY pocket to fix something that was solely his fault. Before he left that night to return to New Jersey, I demanded that he return, preferably when I was out of the house, to repaint the door, molding and door frame. A few days later, I came home from work to a freshly-painted door.

That was the last I would see Mark for quite some time.

· · ·

Trying to communicate with Mark was becoming more and more difficult, which added to my frustration and aggravation. Some days, I would call him two, three, four times. No response. Was he doing it out of spite because I threw him out of the house? The track phone he bought to replace his cell phone confiscated in the raid either had limitations or he was just avoiding my griping. Each time I called him to discuss finances, it was rare that he answered on the first call. His excuse? He was out looking for a job.

One day at work, I escaped to a supply closet where no one would hear me and tried calling Mark, again. This time, he answered. And after I dove into interrogating him about finances, he gave me a sliver of good news.

"I'm expecting a retirement check from the Public School Employees' Retirement System for around $17,000," he said. "It should arrive in the mail soon. You can use that money to help pay for the mortgage, home equity loan, and any other expenses that you can't cover yourself."

I was stunned but at the same time felt this overwhelming sense of relief. *This could get me through several months of mortgage and home equity loan payments, his car payments, insurances—the list went on and on,* I thought. *Manna from heaven.*

Mark was not sharing any updates about what was happening with his criminal case and being in the news business, it seemed unusual that I was not hearing anything either. By the beginning of December, it became clear why. Mark's case was about to take a dramatic turn, but this time, it looked as though I was going to be dragged in as well.

CHAPTER 17

Déjà vu: *(noun, French origin),* a feeling of familiarity or recollection; a feeling of having "already lived through" something.

Once again, in the middle of the workday, my cell phone rang. I glanced at it. I did not recognize the number.

Here we go again, I thought.

I was already deep into writing and producing the 6 o'clock newscast. I watched my phone as it rang a few more times. I was on a deadline, but I answered the call anyway.

"Marisa, I'm a detective with the US Attorney's office in Scranton," a male voice said.

"I'm calling on behalf of the Assistant US Attorney, Michelle Olshefski. We would like to bring you in so we can ask you a few questions about your husband."

I froze for a minute. This was not what I was expecting. I felt blind-sided. *Why on Earth did they want to talk to me?*

"I guess that's possible," I managed to say, the familiar knot tightening in my stomach.

The detective continued, "To avoid any embarrassment with me showing up at WNEP, I can meet you tomorrow morning at 10 a.m. in the parking lot of the restaurant next door to the station for you to sign some documents saying that you agree to be questioned. Is that okay?"

"I guess it is," I answered nervously.

I knew Michelle Olshefski only on a professional basis. She rarely did on-camera interviews, but her name was usually included in press releases pertaining to high-profile criminal cases she prosecuted in United States District Court for the Middle District of Pennsylvania. Although I did not know her personally, I was certainly aware of her reputation as being a tough, no-nonsense federal prosecutor.

After the call, it suddenly dawned on me: Mark's case was being bumped from county to federal court and that explained the nearly month-long inactivity with his case on the county level. It also explained why the FBI was part of the raid at our home in the beginning of November. I figured the reason his case was being taken over by the feds was because the charges and potential punishment are far more severe on the federal level. At this point, the charges he was facing were only on the county level. The affidavit cited a PA code that was a felony 3 - soliciting a minor to engage in a prohibitive sexual act. What I later found out was that since Mark was accused of using a communication device to solicit the minors, it became a federal criminal case rather than state one.

But why me? Why did the feds want to talk with me? I wondered.

More questions. Again with no immediate answers. And yet again, I had to keep my calm, professional, newscaster face on while my insides were churning and as I was preparing to anchor the evening news.

I kept this phone call a big secret from my close friends, co-workers, and yes, even my boss. In the back of my mind, I knew the 2008 document I signed was sitting in my personnel file. I know I had promised to share any new developments. But I was already back to work after the latest hell storm involving Mark, and I did not want anybody, including my news director, to start wondering why the feds wanted to talk with me. It was just too premature. But I did call Mark that day.

"I got a call today from the feds who want to question me about the case against you," I said with very little emotion. "Why do you think they want to talk to me about your case? Do you think they are taking over from Lackawanna County? And if so, why? Does your attorney know anything about this?"

I kept firing one question after another. Mark simply said he did not know but that he would definitely let his attorney know what was going on.

.   .   .

The next morning, I pulled into the near-empty restaurant parking lot. While I waited in my car, I felt like a spy in an undisclosed location, waiting to pass along some super-secret information. Within minutes, a young man pulled up and parked right next to me. We both got out of our cars, and he cordially introduced himself.

He handed me the paper to sign. My hands shook as I read the big, bold print at the top: "Subpoena to testify before a grand jury."

So many questions swirled in my head. *What was I about to sign? Why?* I could not get the questions to move from my brain to my mouth. I needed to sit down to absorb what I was reading. The detective stood patiently near his vehicle while I got back into the front seat of my car glaring at the paper. I read the document again and tried to absorb what it stated.

"You are commanded to appear in this United States district court at the time, date, and place shown below to testify before the court's grand jury." Date and time: December 4, 2012 / 9:30 a.m."

I felt like I had no choice but to sign. So, I reluctantly put my signature on it and gave it to the detective. He thanked me, got back in his car and left.

Again, the only exposure I had to grand juries was through news reports about criminal cases. Grand juries have a certain mystique about them because they are secret proceedings that are meant to gather evidence. It was surreal that here I was, a television news anchorwoman now being called to testify in a criminal case, and not just against anyone, but my own husband!

Then it hit me.

Suppose the feds were after my testimony to see what, if anything, I knew about Mark's communication and relationship with these young guys, but did nothing about it? They could charge ME with conspiracy or obstruction of justice or something to that effect. It would be the big take-down of the big anchorwoman and huge publicity and attention for the U.S. Attorney's office! Several recent local public corruption cases that sent high-profile politicians and judges to prison were proof that the feds are relentless in their pursuit of criminal cases.

So, this was serious, and if the U.S. Attorney's office meant to scare me-- it was successful.

Even in my terrified, frozen state-of-mind, something told me to contact an attorney. Immediately. A close friend of mine who was a paralegal at a local law firm, suggested Daniel Brier, a very reputable defense attorney who worked on some of those high-profile corruption cases in the area. Later that day, I walked into a sound-proof edit booth so no one at work would hear my conversation and called Mr. Brier. He agreed to see me at his downtown Scranton office the following day after I was finished with the 6 o'clock news. I'm grateful he made time for me so quickly. I was ordered to appear before the federal grand jury on Tuesday, December 4th, and I had signed the document on Thursday November 29th.

Our meeting was brief, but informative. Brier explained that because of a legality called spousal privilege, prosecutors cannot force a spouse to testify against a spouse to help prove guilt. The rule applies only to married couples. As far as whether the feds were looking to charge me, Brier was not sure but admitted he did not think so. That put me a little more at ease. He promised to contact Assistant US Attorney Olshefski to let her know why I would not be appearing before Tuesday's grand jury.

"Not to worry," he said as I left the law firm.

That was the last time I had contact with Dan Brier's office until I received a bill for $650. But let me tell you, it was money well spent.

Whether or not federal investigators needed my testimony in Mark's case remains unknown. But one day after I was asked to testify before the federal grand jury, that same jury handed up an indictment against Mark and issued a warrant for his arrest.

CHAPTER 18

"The short answer is you're going to be detained. While you're presumed innocent until proven guilty, the U.S. Congress has determined in certain cases, in certain particularly vile cases and that includes cases that involve minor children, that there is a presumption that they have put in the law that any person who has been charged with those offenses in federal court is presumed to be a danger to the community. A federal grand jury has determined there is in fact probable cause to believe that you have committed the offense against five separate minors."

--U.S. Magistrate Judge Malachy Mannion, December 5, 2012

This is what the federal magistrate stated at Mark's arraignment on charges of online enticement after he turned himself in to federal authorities. The judge denied bail citing the seriousness of the charges. Mark was immediately sent to the Lackawanna County jail where the accused in the county are housed while their criminal cases proceed through the legal system.

Once again, WNEP graciously excused me from work for as long as I felt it was needed.

The pictures of him walking into the federal courthouse on December 5, 2012 were all over the news. That image of him would also be the last time the public would see his face.

Newswatch 16 at 6pm 12/5/2012:

[ANCHOR]

An update tonight on a difficult story for us to report here on Newswatch 16 at 6. The feds have now taken over the child sex abuse case against a man from Lackawanna County, a man we know well.

Newswatch 16's Stacy Lange joins us live from the Lackawanna County Prison in Scranton.

[STACY]

Mark Kandel is locked up here at the Lackawanna County Prison in Scranton without bail now that the FBI has gotten involved in the case that we first told you about last month. Kandel is the husband of Newswatch 16's Marisa Burke. The case against him has now grown. He's accused of having inappropriate contact online with five teenage boys over the last year:

[video story]

Only hours after a federal grand jury handed up an indictment against him, Mark Kandel turned himself in at the federal courthouse in Scranton to face new charges brought on by the FBI.

The child pornography case against the former Lackawanna County educator has grown, and the charges are more serious. In addition to state child pornography charges filed last month, Kandel now faces five federal charges of online enticement.

At his arraignment, US Attorneys said they have evidence that Kandel sent text messages and Facebook messages to five teenage boys where he asked to exchange sexual pictures or massages for money. Prosecutors say they found this evidence after searching Kandel's Peckville home last month and from interviewing the teenage boys and their parents. Detectives say they found 12-thousand text messages sent from Kandel's phone in October alone, 95 percent of them sent to minors. And US Attorneys said when the boys' parents became suspicious, Kandel even bought a cell phone for one of his alleged victims. A federal judge heard some of the details of the case and called Kandel a danger to society. He was sent to prison without bail until his trial scheduled for February. If Kandel is convicted, he faces a possible 50 years in federal prison.

Stacy Lange, Newswatch 16, live from the Lackawanna County Prison in Scranton.

It was mortifying to see and hear my name again all over the news because I was married to this pervert. And this time, the story about Mark's arrest and the fact that he was married to a high-profile anchorwoman was circulated nationally. I was shocked when a friend of mine who lived in the San Francisco area contacted me and said that Mark's story, including my name, was published in their newspaper. All because the Associated Press (AP) picked up the story. Any news outlets with an AP contract can run its stories. I was surprised that Mark's case garnered enough attention that a paper in the San Francisco area had chosen to run it.

But even though I was subjected to all this exposure and embarrassment, for the first time in years, I was not completely devastated. When the state brought charges against Mark the month before, I had made up my mind that I would no longer defend or support him. My conscience refused to allow it. My soul would not allow it. The fact that the feds were taking over Mark's case and filing much more serious charges than what the state was charging him with, reinforced my decision. No pity, no sympathy, no feelings toward him whatsoever.

But I was still angry. Angry at him for putting his family in this position and embarrassing us beyond belief. And angry at myself for being such a fool believing this con man. This time, there was no grieving for him, or for me. It was time to just move on.

And now, I knew I was better off. My girls and I became victims of Mark's betrayal. But instead of feeling defeated, we condemned his actions and it made us stronger. It was finally obvious to my daughters and me that Mark put his perverted desires and gratifications with young guys before his own family. But because we were now distancing ourselves from this liar and con man, I was able to channel my suffering and anguish into defiance and strength.

In the weeks between the time I threw Mark out of the house and when he was incarcerated in December, the girls and I spent most evenings around the dinner table talking about what their father was accused of. Every time we had these conversations, I noticed how the girls were defending their father less and less and criticizing his behavior more and more. Rachael and Sarah were witnesses to how much their father hurt and humiliated me. They saw me break down in tears because the family as we knew it was shattered. They saw the strain on my face. They felt my anguish. They witnessed how Mark's actions threatened my job.

"Mom, we don't blame you for feeling this way," they said to me time and time again. I noticed a transformation with my girls during this time. They were maturing from girls to young women. What happened to their father probably accelerated the process. And when I heard them declare for the first time that they hated their father for what he did, it somehow validated the anger and hostility I had for him. The girls were on my side. The three of us were in agreement, united.

Also, during that time, Rachael and Sarah had auditioned for roles in the musical that Valley View would present in the spring, *West Side Story*. When I got home from work one evening, they were both full of excitement and beaming from ear to ear.

"Mom, we will both be in the show!" they exclaimed with joy. "We need to go out to dinner and celebrate!" We went to their favorite Mexican restaurant. They enthusiastically went into detail how Sarah landed the character of Anita, and Rachael was given the role of a female Glad Hand. Prominent roles! I watched them with delight as they described what it was like being congratulated by their fellow classmates that day. For that hour or so the three of us were simply celebrating together; the madness of what was happening in our personal lives was out of our minds. It was a brief, yet healthy, respite. Then it dawned on me: this would be the first high school musical that Mark would miss.

■　　■　　■

The last time I would cry for Mark occurred the day after he was arraigned.

My close friend Jackie, and my daughter Sarah offered to help me retrieve Mark's vehicle and his personal belongings at his attorney's office in West Scranton. All three of us walked into the building, saying very little because we really did not know what to expect. Mark's lawyer wasn't there, but his legal assistant was. An outdated Formica counter separated her from us. It felt more like I was in an office to pay a bill rather than an attorney's office.

"I'm Marisa Burke. I'm here to collect my husband's belongings," I told her. The woman had me sign the proper papers to release Mark's belongings. These were the items that were on him when he turned himself in to the feds and was then whisked away to jail. None of these things could go with him behind bars.

I was first given Mark's long, navy blue wool overcoat. My mind drifted to the past. I pictured Mark in that beautiful dress coat whenever we were going to a special event or to church. With his six-foot-two stature, he always looked so regal and handsome dressed in that coat. The legal assistant then handed me his wallet. I opened it up. No cash, just a few credit cards, driver's license, health insurance cards, and photos of the girls.

The woman behind the counter finally handed over Mark's wedding band. The gold was somewhat scratched and worn but otherwise in pretty good shape. For some unknown reason, we never had our wedding bands engraved with any kind of messages or initials. Seemed symbolic now that we never did. I stared at the ring as I rolled it around in my hand. My thoughts went back to our wedding day; the moment I placed that ring on his finger, pledging my life-long love and commitment to him before a basilica full of family and friends. It was the happiest day of my life. And from that day forward I never saw Mark without that ring on his finger.

I felt as though I was collecting the personal belongings of a person who had just died, and I began to sob uncontrollably. Sarah started crying as well. Jackie moved closer and put her arm around me.

"Let it out Marisa. It's good to let it out," she said.

The legal assistant stood there, quietly allowing us to deal with this sad moment. I felt overwhelming grief and sorrow, like I would for a death. Not for Mark, but for us. Rachael, Sarah, myself. The survivors of this debacle. The demise of Mark.

Our family had hit rock bottom and the despair was painfully raw. I put the few belongings into a small, clear plastic bag that the legal assistant provided. It was difficult to comprehend that the life of a man who had a successful career in education, married to a popular television news personality, and fathered two sweet girls, was now a plastic bag of personal belongings that were no longer in his possession.

"Do you have the keys to Mark's car," I then asked the woman. "I'm going to try to take it back to the dealer today." She reached behind the counter and handed me the keys.

Mark had parked his bright-blue 2012 Hyundai Veracruz behind the law firm before he and his attorney headed for federal court the day before. My plan was to return the fairly new SUV to the dealership where we bought it in Dickson City, a borough just north of Scranton.

Jackie and Sarah followed me to the parking lot. I was hoping this would be the last time I was in Mark's vehicle. I realized I had to clean out Mark's car before heading to the dealership. He had plastic containers full of insurance policies in the back of the SUV along with other items like an ice scraper, an extra pair of sneakers, and a throw blanket. I removed his insurance and registration cards from the glove compartment and put them in my purse. I collected other miscellaneous items like Triple A road maps and stuffed them into the plastic containers. We packed everything into my car, which Jackie had driven to the dealership.

Returning the SUV did not bother me. I never really liked the vehicle, mainly because of the brand and color Mark had chosen. But after our old minivan started having more and more mechanical problems, Mark came home one day promising he could get a great deal. Like many things, I gave in, and bought the vehicle for him. But with the addition of Rachael's Audi, I was facing three car payments a month and financially that was impractical.

I walked into Dickson City Hyundai along with Jackie and Sarah and explained to the first salesperson who greeted me what the situation was and how I could no longer afford to keep my husband's vehicle.

"We bought this vehicle several months ago for my husband, but we don't need it anymore," I said without giving any more details. I was embarrassed enough being at a dealership, trying to return a car, let alone trying to explain why we no longer needed the car. "I would like to sell the car back to you if that's possible," I continued.

We did not pay cash for the car, but financed it, so I did not think handing back the car would be that much of an issue. The salesperson seemed alarmed when he heard the desperation in my voice and no doubt noticed my disheveled appearance along with my red, swollen eyes. Other customers and salespeople were also looking our way. Despite the pitiful way I looked, I think they recognized me and perhaps were putting two and two together after seeing the news. The salesperson left to speak to someone with higher authority, only to return with disappointing news.

"You'll have to contact corporate offices directly first," he said, "There's nothing we can do for you here today. I'm sorry."

Dejected and defeated, the three of us walked out of the dealership and sat in Mark's vehicle wondering what to do next. But I had no idea what to do. I started to cry again. Jackie and Sarah tried to console me by saying that everything would work out. But I wanted the issue resolved and resolved now. The thought of making a monthly payment on this vehicle was nauseating. Just then, another man came out and asked me to roll down the window so he could talk.

"Marisa, I know what you are going through, and I am so sorry. Come back inside, we will take back the vehicle and you won't have to worry about this anymore," he assured me.

That man, who I presumed was one of the managers, turned out to be the first of many guardian angels who helped me out of the depths of despair. Not only did Hyundai take back Mark's SUV, the dealership handed me a $1,000 check because the vehicle was so new. I never asked how Hyundai came to that amount. I did not care. I was just thrilled I was able to unload the vehicle and another reminder of Mark.

■　　■　　■

Rather than take Mark's case to trial, it appeared as though his attorney was making arrangements to settle on a plea deal with the federal prosecutors. I was exercising in our basement workout room one afternoon in December when my phone rang. It was Mark's attorney. He told me that fighting the charges against Mark would be a long, drawn out process that would double, perhaps even triple, the cost of legal fees. I really did not care what it cost because I was no longer involved in any of Mark's dealings and told him so.

"I really don't know why you're even calling me," I said to him. "I don't really care what happens to Mark at this point. So, if he has to plead guilty because he doesn't have enough money to go to trial, then let him plead guilty."

Later that December, Mark's retirement check arrived in the mail. Right there in bold and beautiful numbers: $17,625.34. I thought, *let me put both Mark's signature and mine on the check and get it in the bank fast. It will be the cushion I need to pay expenses, mortgage and home equity loan payments—exactly what we discussed over the phone the month before.*

It was unrealistic to expect any more money from Mark now that he was indefinitely behind bars. The next morning, I got up early and hurriedly drove to my credit union in Bloomsburg and deposited the check. I felt as though I was trying to bury hidden treasure.

I got back into the car breathing a huge sigh of relief. But leave it to Mark to say something to appease me that turned out to be a lie. I assume he promised his defense attorney that he, too, could use that money for legal expenses. He also must have given his attorney the heads-up that the check was mailed because of what happened next.

A few days later when I arrived home from work, the girls told me they looked out the window that afternoon and saw Mark's attorney sitting in his car in front of our house, waiting for the mail to arrive. Again, I presumed that Mark had given him permission to take the check addressed to him from the Public School Employees' Retirement System, maybe as a retainer fee. Another piece of evidence that showed exactly how sinister Mark was. Luck was on my side that I was able to intercept the check first. *Let Mark figure out another way to pay his defense attorney,* I said to myself. It was not like I was using the money to go on a trip to Europe. I used that money to survive.

■　　■　　■

What would Christmas be like this year for Rachael and Sarah without their father? I wondered. A season that I had always looked forward to with the giddiness of a child; one that symbolized joy and love instead brought me to tears after Mark's arrest and incarceration.

Christmas was always so special for us as a family. In the weeks leading up to it, I spent every spare moment outside of work decorating our home, buying and wrapping the girls' gifts and preparing and planning for all the traditional holiday meals.

My goal was always to make Christmas as memorable for the girls as it had been for my brothers and me growing up when our parents went all out with decorating. Our childhood home always had candles in the windows, garland on the picket fence, a spotlight on the door illuminating a beautiful wreath that my mother crafted herself. Our colonial-themed decorations were so attractive that one year, *The Danville News* took a picture and published it in the newspaper. My parents, especially my mother, reveled in the fact that their home stood out in the neighborhood and was widely admired.

Decorating our tree each year was a Christmas highlight because it was a time to reminisce about our family vacations and special times we spent together. Most of our ornaments were souvenirs representing the special places we had been. We also set aside a night every December to watch the animated movie "Polar Express" where we all cuddled up on the couch in the basement with the fireplace on, sipping hot chocolate and savoring the pepperoni bread I always baked for the holidays.

Before Mark was incarcerated and while he was staying with his brother in New Jersey, I talked with the girls about the holidays. They were visibly upset about the possibility of being separated from him on Christmas. So, I wanted to comfort them without opening the door wide for him.

"I don't see any harm in having your father spend Christmas Day here," I said. "But it is only for one day. Nothing more."

As it turned out, Mark was incarcerated without bail in early December so there was no chance he would be free for the holiday.

How could I possibly make this year's Christmas happy for the girls under these ugly and unforeseen circumstances? The entire scenario was heartbreaking. What an extreme contrast from past holidays that were always filled with such joy, anticipation, and excitement.

My brother Chris and his wife Nancy turned out to be the next guardian angels. They insisted that the girls and I spend Christmas and New Year's in Michigan with their family. "The diversion will do the girls some good," they said. I knew it would be a way for the girls and me to leave behind this mess and salvage some sort of holiday spirit.

Accepting my brother's invitation was one of the best decisions I ever made. I wrapped the girls' gifts, packed them in boxes and shipped them to Michigan so they would arrive in time for the holiday. On the day before Christmas Eve, we packed the car, picked up my mother and headed west.

My brother's children and Rachael and Sarah were all around the same age, and whenever the girls got together with their Michigan cousins, they always had a wonderful time. My brother and sister-in-law live in a lovely two-story colonial home on the outskirts of Ann Arbor and they, too, always made sure that Christmas for their children was a magical time filled with traditions. They went above and beyond that year to accommodate the girls and me, and for that, I will be forever grateful.

We attended Christmas Eve mass with my brother's family, my mom, and the girls. The church was beautifully decorated and packed with families dressed in their best holiday attire. Everybody looked so happy, and I tried to put on the best face for my girls. But deep inside, I felt so distant, so alone, and was filled with so much pain. By this time, I was physically and emotionally drained. *How could that man have ruined our holiday the way he did,* I kept saying to myself over and over in my head.

I was also thinking about how Mark was spending his Christmas Eve behind bars. *Does the jail have any kind of special meal? How much was he longing for his family? His girls? Was he depressed? Was he crying? I hoped he was crying. I hoped he was hurting. God, I hoped he was hurting. I hoped he was sitting in his cell thinking about how he blew it. With me and his girls. I hoped he was feeling the same excruciating pain and loneliness I was feeling at that moment. I had not one ounce of pity for him.* In my mind, I called him an idiot. A fucking idiot.

Then I realized where I was - during Christmas Eve Mass, feeling awful and vindictive, when everyone else around me was celebrating. But even being in church during a time of religious celebration could not pull me out of the fog of my situation.

Rachael and Sarah had a blast with their cousins that Christmas. Being away from northeastern Pennsylvania was not only a good distraction, but I believe it saved the three of us from being sucked into a hole of despair. Michigan was the life jacket we needed at that time. To this day, the girls say the Christmas of 2012 was the best Christmas they ever had. How about that irony...

CHAPTER 19

On our way back from our holiday vacation in Michigan, we stopped at a travel center along the Ohio Turnpike when my phone rang. It was Mark's attorney, but since I was in a bathroom stall, I let the call go to voicemail. Fortunate for me, I did.

"Marisa, you went ahead and took Mark's retirement check. That money was meant for me. It was too late to put a stop payment on it so I expect you to give the money back or I'm going to the authorities and saying that you fraudulently signed his name on the check."

How dare he threaten me. Worse still, how dare Mark use what money he had—on an attorney and not his family! My defenses went up even more. I knew in my heart that money belonged to me and should be used to support the girls. Mark's criminal behavior had thrust us into a desperate situation. And as the saying goes, *desperate times call for desperate measures.* My desperate measure was depositing his retirement check. *So, go to the authorities,* I thought. I was ready for a challenge and a fight. My argument would have been that Mark told me in November I could use the money to pay bills. I ignored the attorney's phone call, and he never called back. It was the last time, the retirement check ever came up—in conversation.

My next guardian angel appeared in my life in January 2013 and came through a good family friend. Torrey Sattof was Mark's mentor and colleague at Banker's Life and Casualty. He would often meet Mark at our house and then they would head out together for work appointments at people's homes. He also became a good friend of the family. Torrey was going through a divorce and had no children of his own. So, when he was at the house, he really enjoyed spending time with Rachael and Sarah.

Right before Christmas Torrey reached out to see if I needed anything. He also wanted me to meet a friend of his.

"I have a lawyer friend name Jennifer Hadley," he said. "I would love for you to talk with her. She is really down to earth and is a brilliant woman."

Torrey promised that she would be a beacon for advice and guidance during this very difficult adjustment time. We arranged to meet at his house in Swoyersville, about a 25-minute drive south from Scranton, on that cold January Saturday afternoon.

Jennifer was already there when I arrived. She was a younger woman, casually dressed, with long, wavy blonde hair. The three of us sat down and spent several minutes in small talk - going over our backgrounds, what we did for a living, what we liked to do in our spare time.

And then Torrey brought up Mark. Jennifer was a former assistant district attorney in Luzerne County, so she was familiar with Mark's criminal case. She seemed curious about certain aspects of the case and thought it was significant that the feds took over the investigation from the state. But then, she said something that came out of nowhere.

"You need to divorce Mark as quickly as possible," she explained. "You need to do this to show your family, your friends, your employer, your viewers, and the feds that you are committed to breaking ties with this person."

Up until that moment, "divorce" was something I thought I could tackle months down the road when things calmed down, and I knew that Rachael and Sarah were okay with the idea. Right now, I was so focused on protecting the girls and doing everything I could to keep some sort of normalcy in their lives. Consequently, when Jennifer encouraged me to file for divorce sooner than later, it was like she threw a bucket of cold water right in my face and yelled "wake up!"

She also ended up playing counselor and psychologist that day in between my crying sessions. Jennifer never charged me for her consultation. And it turned out that hers was some of the most worthwhile advice I ever received. I never saw her or spoke to her again after our visit that day. She was an angel who made a brief appearance, gave me a message and disappeared. We did connect on LinkedIn a few years later, exchanged one brief message and that was it.

. . .

After the first of the year, the girls started receiving hand-written letters from their father while he was in jail. You would think that the letters would be full of remorse, apologizing profusely for all he had done, for betraying us the way he did. But they sounded more like letters between pen pals.

Dear Rachael and Sarah,

Happy Valentine's Day! I hope this letter finds you well. How is school going? Daddy is doing ok. How is swimming? You must be near the end of your season. What is your record? What events are you both swimming? I had a very quiet birthday on February 1st. My two cellmates made me a birthday card. At lunch, many of the guys gave me their desserts as a gift.

Dear Rachael and Sarah,

Happy Easter! I assume you still have your long Easter break even with the snow today. How is school going? Do you like your classes this semester? I assume you are going to Nana's for Easter. May all of you have a wonderful and blessed holiday. I won't write anymore for a while, since I haven't heard from you over the past four months. I hope as the days, weeks, months, and years pass, you will remember all of the good things I have done for you, as well as all of the happy memories. I love you both very much and will continue to ask God to bless you and guide you. My love always, Daddy xxooxx

What the fuck? was all I could think after reading them. The letters sounded so juvenile, and like he was writing to them while away on a business trip rather than in jail. I just could not believe it! Nonetheless, I offered to keep the lines of communication open.

"If you want to write back to your father, I have the address at the jail," I told them.

Neither one wanted anything to do with corresponding with their dad.

During our January conversation, Jennifer Hadley had also recommended a friend of hers to be my divorce attorney. Even though Greg Skibitsky's law practice was in the Pittston area of neighboring Luzerne County and not Lackawanna, she urged me to contact him because he had a reputation for being one of the best divorce attorneys in Luzerne County.

Greg's law office was nothing fancy, but it proved to me that you do not need opulent offices to impress. He was neither flamboyant, loud nor obnoxious, which are some adjectives I have often seen used to stereotype divorce lawyers. He was a very gentle, sincere individual who clearly put his client's best interests first. I was at ease before walking into the conference room to meet with him.

He pulled out a legal pad and began the questioning. How long were we married? How many children, their ages? Did we own our home? All relevant details for a lawyer planning out a divorce. And when attorneys start listing marital assets and marital debt, you quickly realize that marriage is not all about love. What it is really all about is a legal contract.

And "divorce" is the process by which you break that contract. I sat there thinking that the husband who betrayed me and his family did not deserve one dime after what he did to us. Receiving anything was a disgrace in my book. I also thought that if Mark were a decent father, he would just walk away and allow me to use the marital estate to help raise our daughters and put them through college. Custody of the girls was obviously not an issue since Mark was incarcerated. But Greg made it very clear I stood to lose a lot of money since I was the one who made more money during our marriage. The thought of that made my stomach turn.

Greg walked me through all of the scenarios that could happen with a divorce, which included having a judge decide the split if both parties are in total disagreement. He wanted me to be prepared. Right then, I promised myself I would fight for the sake of the future of our daughters.

At the end of February 2013, Greg filed the divorce petition on my behalf and notified Mark:

Dear Mr. Kandel,

Please be advised that this office has been retained to represent your wife, Marisa Burke-Kandel in connection with the above referenced divorce action with the Lackawanna County Court of Common Pleas. Enclosed please find a Complaint in Divorce and Notice to Defend and Claim Rights which were filed on February 28, 2013.

Around the same time, Torrey dropped another bomb. To plan for retirement, I had rolled over money from an old 401K into an annuity with Banker's. The policy was solely in my name, but it was Mark who actually had done all the paperwork when he was still a Banker's employee. Torrey asked whether I knew about the money that Mark had withdrawn from my annuity back in November of 2011. I had no idea what he was talking about. Mark had forged my name to withdraw $13,798.00! It suddenly became clear how Mark still had money between the time he quit Banker's and supposedly went to work for New York Life. He stole a significant amount of money from me, and passed it off as his own money. The money he was still giving me for his half of the mortgage and the home equity loan—was actually *my* money that he withdrew from *my* annuity! I was not only a victim of betrayal but now a victim of fraud. The hurt of it all was agonizing. *He really didn't care about me at all,* I kept thinking over and over in my head.

As if it were not bad enough that he was accused of crimes against minors, he was now a con man, thief, swindler, and cheat. And again, I was in the cross-hairs. This was hard-earned money I had put aside for my retirement. He must have had balls the size of Montana to secretly reach into my account and steal money! *My God,* I thought. How could he have been so hateful, deceitful and selfish? Yet another gut punch! My anger for him was churning like a newly formed tropical storm.

But it was also the motivation I needed to follow through on what Jennifer advised me to do: divorce the son of the bitch and put this nightmare behind me as quickly as possible. There was no reason to rage about the stolen retirement money. It was gone. And there was nothing I could do about it.

Mark decided to use his criminal attorney to represent him in the divorce. And as much as I thought this would be a slam-dunk considering that he was incarcerated, I was wrong. Mark's attorney filed a countersuit and soon after, the emails, letters, and faxes started flying back and forth between the two lawyers.

Frank was still stinging after not receiving the money from Mark's retirement check and was threatening to contact the State Attorney General's office over allegations I committed fraud signing Mark's check. My attorney went on the offensive with a letter in response:

Mr. Kandel's conduct alone has left Marisa in a financially precarious situation without any financial contribution from him which has required her to be the sole means of support for her household and the parties' teenage daughters. Surely you can appreciate the parties' financial obligations, their mortgage alone being $3,000 per month, were difficult to maintain because of Mr. Kandel's past conduct and are even more so now that Marisa must meet said obligations without any contribution from Mr. Kandel. Marisa maintains that Mr. Kandel was more than aware of her actions relative to the PSERS check in question. Marisa maintains that both she and Mr. Kandel each during their entire course of their marriage on many occasions, endorsed checks made payable to the other for deposit into their joint accounts. If Mr. Kandel is now to attribute conduct to Marisa, she must remind him that he himself has made withdrawals from Marisa's annuity, unbeknownst to her, and endorsed checks copying her signature in order to pay his bills.

Touché. Boom. Out for the count. Game, set and match. Checkmate. Take your choice. Threatening to take legal action against me over Mark's retirement check never came up in any correspondence again.

CHAPTER 20

The chances of Mark being released from jail now were either slim or none. So, I decided to clear out his belongings at the house. The walk-in closet was first. In front of me were a row of suits. I touched his ties and counted the designer dress shirts commercially pressed on hangars.

I tried not to get knocked over by the alternating waves of sadness and anger. *He certainly won't need any of these in prison,* I thought. I offered up Mark's classic suits, dress shirts, and ties to my co-anchor who was about Mark's height and had a similar build.

"Whatever is there, is there for the taking," I said to him. One Saturday afternoon he came to the house and took a few suits and some shirts. The rest I gave to other guys I knew and whatever was left over ended up at the Salvation Army. Whether it was dressers full of clothes, nightstands filled with inspirational books or shelves cluttered with mementos of years gone by, emptying everything and tossing out proved cathartic. There was a lot of bad energy in that house and as we headed into summer, my mission was to cleanse, purge and purify what I could.

Up next on the list? Mark's office. His office was his domain. He is the one who picked the executive-style cherry desk, cherry bookshelves he filled with academic books and a leather-bound collection of Agatha Christie novels, a cushioned black leather office chair that matched the décor and a few accent lamps. Factor in the flat-screen TV and a stereo, and it was no wonder Mark would hole up in his office for hours at a time. I never had a reason to be in

153

there, and I respected Mark's privacy whenever he had the paned glass doors shut. But now the office was mine.

I tackled the desk first. And I certainly wasn't prepared for what I found. One drawer was filled with receipts for Calvin Klein men's underwear, sneakers and gym shorts. Everything that was mentioned in the affidavits. There were dozens of other receipts for shopping excursions and restaurants, none of which I could connect to any family outings. He obviously thought that by hiding these receipts in his desk, I would never find them.

These were difficult to discover, but the worst was yet to come in another drawer. I was sifting through what appeared to be miscellaneous papers when I came across a print-out of a conversation from an on-line chat room. Mark's moniker was "Pecman from PA." The following is the conversation with names omitted to protect their identities:

Pecman from PA:
"Are you bisexual?"
"You must know the_____ twins."
IamAchilles:
"_____ and_____?"
PecmanfromPA:
"yeah."
"I always thought_____ was bi – u guys looking for a 3rd?"
IamAchilles:
"Who is this?"
PecmanfromPA:
"A friend of the twins. Bi here too. It's cool dude. I am married and discrete. So u need not worry."

My stomached churned.

Online chat rooms lost their popularity when Facebook came on the scene, so it was obvious this conversation had taken place several years ago. Why law enforcement never confiscated this printout or any of the receipts when they raided our home in November was baffling. Then again, they were probably concentrating their search on Mark's electronics and more importantly, his cell phone.

Nonetheless, there were the receipts that verified what was in Mark's arrest papers, along with a repugnant chat room conversation that reinforced my worst suspicions: I married a man who, from the very beginning, was pretending to be someone he was not. He used me, his trophy wife, to hide his true sexuality and his perverted attraction to young guys. He tricked me into thinking I was marrying a heterosexual man.

How could I have been so stupid? What other warning signs did I miss? Why was I not like other wives who, every so often, pried into their husband's personal space or spied on their phones. I was mad at myself for being so foolish and naïve. I could have asked Mark years ago when sex between us was getting less and less. I put blinders on because I was determined to protect my personal and public life. I did not want anything to tarnish my job that brought notoriety and prestige. I did not want anything to ruin that image we had of being the perfect family leading the perfect life. A life my parents had raising their three children.

What kind of charade was I playing to make it seem like life was grand and why was I not more honest and truthful with myself when things went sour? I grapple with these questions to this day. What is so sad, is that I may never come up with the right answers.

My stomach was in knots as I continued to clean. I felt as though the entire office needed to be disinfected with Lysol and Clorox. As I started sifting through a filing cabinet, I made another discovery that Mark kept hidden from me: several legal-size envelopes mailed to him that were full of correspondence from the Commonwealth of Pennsylvania Department of Education. I knew after he pleaded guilty in 2008 to furnishing alcohol to minors that he eventually lost his education certification in Pennsylvania. But because I was so side-tracked with trying to maintain normalcy for the girls and protect my career, I was too distracted to inquire about the details of the 'how' behind the Commonwealth of PA removing Mark's certification. And now, here it was right in front of me.

I learned that the Department had conducted its own investigation into what happened in accordance with the Professional Educator Discipline Act. In a letter dated May 5, 2009 from the Office of Chief Counsel, it talked about the original complaint that Mark hosted a party for teenagers from the year before and served them alcohol. But the department learned of allegations that Mark engaged in additional acts of misconduct and a second complaint was filed against him. The second complaint alleged that Mark gave gifts of underwear to teens, made inappropriate inquiries of a sexual nature to teens, offered teenagers money to pose for pictures just wearing underwear, and gave a male student a wet/dry shaver, invited him to shave at our home and had inappropriate pictures on his home computer. Everything he denied to me during his first round of trouble with the law or dismissed as "locker room humor."

But here is what I found even more alarming. Toward the end of May 2009, the department filed a notice of its own version of 'charges' to Mark by certified mail. On June 1 and 5, 2009, the post office delivered Mark the notice by certified mail. But by June 17, the post office sent back the notice to the Department of Education, marked as unclaimed.

In other words, Mark ignored all notices from the Department of Education, failed to respond to any of the accusations leveled against him from the state, and never signed any papers relinquishing his certification. In response, the state issued an order dated October 27, 2009 that the professional educator certification issued to Mark W. Kandel was REVOKED—in all capital letters. The Commonwealth of Pennsylvania would never allow Mark to teach students ever again.

I finally understood that the process of Mark losing his certification did not happen overnight. It was an involved, year-long process. Several people were looped in the investigation, including all the board members of Northeast Intermediate Unit #19 who were copied on all the correspondence. But again, I was left blind-sided. He never shared any of this with me.

After discovering this paperwork, I could only conclude one of two things: he knew the state accusations against him were true and did not want me to know about it, or he just no longer cared about teaching in Pennsylvania. Either way, I could not fathom how this man who spent so much time and energy pursuing a doctorate in education, could just throw away his career.

■　　■　　■

Bit by bit, I removed signs of Mark from the house. His clothes. The contents of his office. I even got rid of the antique chifforobe and love seat in our bedroom that were his before we got married. All of it—gone. It was the cleansing I so desperately needed to get rid of his ugliness.

Then came the photos.

Our home was filled with family photos. Most of them were of the girls themselves. But others were family portraits taken by professional photographers. The portraits that included Mark, all came down. My impulse was to throw them out. But for now, I thought, I would just put them in storage. As long as they were off the walls and somewhere I didn't have to see them.

Next to come down was the beautifully framed wedding portrait of me hanging in our formal living room and my wedding bouquet that was dried and pressed into an oval brown antique frame. By this time, neither Rachael nor Sarah had anything good to say about their father. They supported my decision to take down the photos and remove any mementos that reminded them of their dad.

We wanted no traces of the ghost of Mark. So next, came cleansing with sage. I had often read about saging, which is a Native-American ritual to cleanse a person, place or object of negative energy. You light a sage stick, then blow it out so that the embers still glow and smoke. Then you move around the home, allowing the smoke to drift as it cleanses and empties out past energies. Saging is supposed to be good to do during times of change.

Around this time, I wanted another dog as a companion for my Molly. I am a firm believer in adopting rescue dogs, so through an online search, I found Cindy Sadler, who ran a rescue shelter about 30 miles from Scranton. She found me a black lab mix named Patsy. As it turned out, Cindy was also a firm believer in saging.

Cindy and I hit it off the moment I met her. She was twice divorced, living alone and was the same age. She lived a somewhat Bohemian lifestyle, believed in astrology and searched for meanings in horoscopes. We often had conversations about the turmoil I was going through, and she kindly offered to help with the transition in my life.

"How 'bout I stop by for a visit and sage your home?" she said. "I really think it will do some good, and help you move on."

So one afternoon Cindy brought a stock of dried white sage to the house. After she lit it, we walked from room to room, wafting the smoke where walls met ceilings, through windows and doorways. We started on the first floor, then headed upstairs to the bedrooms. Then we headed downstairs to the basement.

"Oh my!" she suddenly exclaimed. "I am suddenly feeling a sense of heaviness. Negative, creepy energy. I am really feeling it in your weight room. And I'm feeling the same thing over by your red, sectional couch down here."

All I could think of at that moment was what Mark admitted to investigators: that "he allowed teenage boys to go to his house at night where he would allow them to enter through a basement door so that no one else in the house would know that they were there."

God only knows what happened in the basement with those boys, late at night/early in the morning, I thought. All those nights he came to bed around 2 or 3 a.m. saying he had fallen asleep in the basement watching TV. What really happened? What kind of activity was taking place on the red couch? What was going on in the weight room? I had disgusting, salacious images in my head of young guys, with their shirts off, perhaps lifting weights, and Mark jerking off nearby. It made me sick. I wanted Cindy to be the exorcist to cast out the demon, the devil-- to cast out Mark in hopes that his lecherous behavior would become a distant memory.

CHAPTER 21

At some point after Mark was charged by the feds, Torrey told me something that I have held on to ever since. The wisdom was especially appropriate considering the chaos in my life at the time: "If you surround yourself with good people, only good things will happen to you."

One of those good people continued to be David, who has been my closest friend for more than 30 years. When Mark left the picture in December of 2012, David willingly stepped in to see how he could help around the house and offer emotional support any way he could. He was always there to listen to my rants about how Mark ruined our lives. He encouraged me to remain positive, insisting my wounds would heal in time. These conversations usually occurred outside work, when we enjoyed some down time together either at his house or after dinner I made at home. Sometimes I would think about Mark and freak out simply during a drive to the movies. But that was okay with David. He allowed me to vent my frustration, aggravation, and bitterness.

I was attracted to his intellect in so many ways. Not only is he one of the best news writers I know, he can build, fix, or figure out just about anything. He was never one to dive deep into a conversation about politics, but he would always jump at a chance to YouTube a mechanical problem to find a way to fix it. He knew practical things, and he built his lake-front home himself.

His skills with tools and knowledge about construction came in handy in 2013. Because of course, as if it were not challenging enough having my husband in jail, major parts of the house started breaking. Microwave, garbage disposal, pool heater and filter, garage door opener - even the furnace and air conditioning system! Dave was eager to repair most everything in the house. The only thing out of his wheelhouse was the furnace and AC unit. He saved me a lot of money at a time when I really did not have it.

■　　■　　■

I confided in David during this time when I was trying to keep my head above water financially. I had very little breathing room. When you count on your spouse to fill in the budget gaps and then suddenly that income disappears, it's the scariest thing in the world. I cut back on other expenses, contributed less to my 401K, and limited the times we went out to dinner.

But it never fails. Just when you think you are caught up with paying the bills and fulfilling your financial responsibilities so that you may have a little more money to play with, something else breaks down or your children need something, and you are back to where you started from: making sure there's enough money between paychecks. The furnace and air conditioning system cost close to $5,000 to replace. Other things continued to break down at the house, and Rachael's Audi turned out to be very high maintenance with a long list of expensive repairs. The pattern of misfortunes and mishaps served as a metaphor of what my life was like at the moment.

You learn to swallow your pride and do anything you need to do to stay above water. That's what I did.

For years, Mark and I dropped loose change into a clear, glass chemical jug that sat in the corner of our bedroom. We always said it would someday be our vacation money to Hawaii. But sadly, I needed the money for the house, not to jet off on a dream vacation. And I needed it fast. The jug itself was way too heavy to haul into a bank, so Dave and I dumped the coins into buckets and loaded them into his pickup truck. We carried them, two by two, into PNC Bank in Peckville. It took several minutes, to dump all the quarters, dimes, nickels and pennies into the coin machine. All the while, people in the bank were staring because they recognized who I was. It did not matter. We were on a mission.

Fortunately Dave was there to cushion the embarrassment. I ended up with just over $500, which enabled me to make a home equity loan payment!

After our trip to the bank, we headed for a jewelry store. I had no use for our wedding bands and my engagement ring, so I figured this could be another opportunity for quick cash. Both wedding bands were 14-carat gold and diamonds were inlaid in my ring. My engagement ring was simple, a round cut not even a half-carat, with two triangular-shaped diamonds on each side. Even though the ring was nothing extravagant or fancy, I had treasured that ring and the memory of the day Mark proposed on the beach in Florida.

But those rings did not matter anymore. They meant nothing. They represented a part of my life that I was now trying to run from as far and fast as I could. Pawning those rings would help detach myself from Mark. I glanced at the rings one more time before handing them over to the jeweler who ended up estimating their value much lower than what I thought, about $700. Talk about disappointing. But again, I was too embarrassed to argue for more money because the jeweler knew who I was. If I had pursued the issue further, it would have made me look like some degenerate pawning valuables to get money for something seedy. Everything felt so wrong.

■　　■　　■

By the middle of March, my divorce filing was published in *The Scranton Times-Tribune*. The legal notice was proof to everyone, including my bosses at WNEP, that I was serious about breaking my allegiance to this man I called my husband for 18 years. It also meant removing my name from any and all future news stories about him. WNEP-TV never connected me with Mark again in any other news reports.

Coincidentally, the weekend my divorce was announced in the newspaper, just happened to be the weekend of Valley View's musical production of *West Side Story* in which both Rachael and Sarah had leading roles. Since the show is about ethnic intimidation and learning to accept and tolerate cultural differences, the drama directors had asked me to speak to the audiences before each performance about bullying in school. Getting up and speaking before large groups of people does not bother me. But knowing that many of those people in the audience that weekend had probably just seen my divorce announcement in the paper was a bit intimidating and unsettling.

The last thing I wanted under these circumstances was to bring any more attention to myself, but to my surprise, the warm reception and applause when I got up on stage was heartfelt and genuine. The entire experience was the confidence-booster I needed at a time when my personal life felt like a free fall with a faulty parachute and no safety net.

CHAPTER 22

By now Mark was dealing with both a criminal case and a divorce proceeding against him. Perhaps the frustration over not hearing from his daughters was building because in late spring, I received a notice from Lackawanna County Family Court that practically shot me to the moon:

"You, Marisa Burke-Kandel, the Plaintiff, have been sued in Court to obtain custody, partial custody, or visitation of the children, Rachael and Sarah Kandel. You, as a parent, are directed to attend the "Kids First" seminar on the assigned date listed below: June 18, 2013."

Kids First is an educational program designed for families to help their children cope with divorce. Parents learn how parental conflict can have a direct effect on children. My blood was boiling. As I later learned from Greg, this mandate from Lackawanna County was part of Mark's assertion of a count for custody in his divorce counterclaim. He desperately wanted me to drag the girls to jail to see him, and he thought by forcing me into a custody conference, this would occur.

"He is their father and deserves to see his girls," was in the letter my divorce attorney received from Mark's counsel.

But my attorney made it very clear that the girls did NOT want to see their father while he was behind bars and that Rachael and Sarah were certainly old enough to make these decisions on their own. So, forcing me to take part in a Kids First program was moot.

Even so, I thought, *the audacity of this fucking monster to think that he could strong-arm his girls into seeing him. And for what? To ask how their school year went?* Besides that, I was totally against exposing Rachael and Sarah to a jail setting.

Mark's divorce attorney was not about to give up so easily. Frank was not convinced until he talked with the girls himself and he wanted to talk with them somewhere, in person.

"Let's appease him and your husband by agreeing to this," Greg advised me. We agreed, under certain conditions. Mark must agree to honor and abide by the girls' decision, whatever that may be. Should the girls determine they do not wish to see their father while he is incarcerated, he must agree to cease and desist in pursuing his custody claim.

On the day before I was scheduled to attend the Kids First seminar, I reluctantly took the girls to Greg's office to talk about visiting their father in jail. I was not allowed to be in the meeting with them. But as I parked the car, I told them to listen to what the lawyers had to say, but that they were free to make their own decision.

The meeting lasted about 30 minutes. I could hear Frank's boisterous voice through the wall in a room next door but could not make out what he was saying. When Frank was leaving, I heard him wish the girls well. Then my attorney walked into the room where I was waiting.

"You won't have to attend a Kids First seminar or a custody conference," Greg said with satisfaction. "The girls made it absolutely clear they do not want to see their father now nor anytime in the future."

June 4, 2013. The day the U.S. Attorney's office announced that a plea deal was filed that day in federal court. Mark agreed to plead guilty to one count of online enticement of minors. But the developments that day presented a very unique situation for me at Newswatch 16: do I leave work or stay? Since I filed for divorce, I knew that my name would no longer be connected to any of Mark's stories. But how would I anchor the 6 o'clock newscast, knowing that one of the stories was about Mark? Even though we were separated, it would have been extremely awkward to read the story of his plea agreement on air.

Fortunately, I was also the producer of the 6 p.m. newscast, which meant I not only wrote the stories, but I also determined where to place the stories in the newscast and which anchor read which story. I decided to craft the newscast with my co-anchor reading the story about Mark's plea agreement. I also had my partner read several other stories that followed in the sequence, to allow for enough "buffer" between the time Mark's story aired and when I was back on camera.

The newscast choreography worked so well that I used the same strategy when Mark was back in court at the end of the month to plead guilty. I stayed on the air, despite the plea agreement being a major news story.

Date: June 25, 2013
Change of Plea
Federal Court Wilkes-Barre, PA

JUDGE: All right. Now, I'm going to read to you the elements of the offense and ask you whether or not you're guilty of those elements. First, that you knowingly used, in this case, a computer and a cellular device in interstate commerce to attempt to persuade, induce, entice an individual under the age of 18 years to engage in sexual activity as charged in count one of the indictment; secondly, that you believe that such individual was less than 18 years of age; third, that if sexual activity had occurred you could have been charged with a criminal offense under the law of Pennsylvania; and, fourth, that you acted knowingly and willfully. Those are the four elements of the offense. Are you guilty of each of these four elements?

KANDEL: Yes, sir.

Judge: All right. Now I am going to ask Ms. Olshefski to outline in summary form the facts that would meet these elements, and I will ask you to listen carefully because I will ask you whether or not you agree with what she said.

MS. OLSHEFSKI: Your honor, on November 7th 2012, the defendant was arrested by Detective Justin Leri of the Lackawanna County District Attorney's Office, and he was charged at that time with criminal solicitation to produce child pornography and unlawful contact. Detective Leri had been familiar with Mr. Kandel from a prior investigation dating back to May 2008. As part of the evidence that the government would establish at trial, Mr. Kandel pled guilty to charges related to that activity in 2008 but his conduct in relation to minors did not stop. And, if fact, Detective Leri continued to receive complaints about the defendant involving inappropriate online relationship with minors, and those complaints received were dating from 2008 through 2012.

On November 1st, 2012, Detective Leri was contacted by a 17-year-old male who stated that he had been involved in text message communications with the defendant. He stated that the text messages were very perverted. He stated, and he would testify in this court although he continued to go along with him for a while, he became nervous as the messaging became more sexual in nature. The 17-year-old male provided Detective Leri with a screen shot of text messages and an image.

The image was sent to him by the defendant, and the image depicted the defendant wearing compression underwear which appeared to focus on the crotch area of the defendant. The 17-year-old male was further interviewed by Detective Leri on November 2nd, the very next very day with his parents present.

He would testify that he met the defendant through his friends and that the defendant offered to help him with his school work. The minor would testify that he communicated with the defendant through email and text messages. He would testify that at first the conversations were harmless but then quickly became sexual in nature and that he was nervous but continued to go along with the defendant. At one point, however, at the request of the defendant, the minor was going to provide the defendant with nude pictures of himself in exchange for money and/or other favors. The minor would testify that the defendant asked to meet with him on several occasions for what the minor believed was going to be a sexual encounter of some kind.

At that time, the minor told Detective Leri that he did not delete any of the text messages despite the fact that the defendant had advised him to delete everything. Detective Leri immediately performed a forensic extraction of the minor's cell phone and noted in excess of 900 messages between the defendant and the minor in just the month of October 2012.

The messages began with a discussion of the defendant helping the minor with his college entry essay but quickly progressed into sexual connotations including asking what type of underwear the minor liked to wear, what size his penis was and what his pubic grooming habits were. Throughout the messages, the defendant referred to the age of the juvenile and repeatedly asked when he would turn 18.

At first the defendant agreed to accept pictures of the juvenile in lieu of physical conduct, but then he persisted in trying to arrange physical meeting with the minor. The text messages are explicit and unequivocal with respect to what the defendant was hoping to obtain. Obviously, those text messages would be displayed to a jury. Several times during the month of October, the defendant and the minor discussed transferring sexually explicit pictures of the minor to the defendant on either a CD or a memory card. And in referring to the transfer of pictures, the conversations include the minor being compensated for the pictures.

Text messages also revealed multiple instances of the defendant wanting to meet the juvenile including visits to his workplace and at his school, and in other instances the defendant discussed meeting with the juvenile for front and back massages. On November 5, 2012, a search warrant was executed on the defendant's residence in Peckville, and multiple computer-related items were seized including the defendant's cell phone.

The defendant was Mirandized, and he was interviewed by Detective Leri. And during the interview he admitted that he does engage in sexual conversations with teenage boys through his cell phone and also through Facebook, and Facebook records were obtained, and they were consistent with text messages and would also be part of the government's proof at trial. The defendant stated that he considers himself a mentor for teenage boys and further admitted that the sexual messages have some truth to them and that he becomes overwhelmed with sexual feelings during the process.

The defendant admitted to Detective Leri that he would often buy gifts for many different juveniles such as clothes, cell phone, car parts, video games or simply give them cash. He admitted to frequently taking them to restaurants and purchasing other gifts for them, and he admitted to Detective Leri that he frequently allowed teenage boys to go to his house at night where he would allow them to enter through a basement door so that no one else in the house would know that they were there. The defendant's admissions would be offered in addition to the testimony of the minors at trial.

And the minors would testify that in addition to what the defendant admitted, he also provided them with alcohol on a regular basis, and he routinely purchased Calvin Klein underwear for them and asked them to model the underwear for him. He would provide Speedo bathing suits for swimming at his house where he would also provide the alcohol. Detective Leri would testify about the forensic examination of the defendant's cell phone and the extraction of in excess of 13,000 text messages between the defendant and at least 17 additional juvenile males. Those messages would cover the span of only a few months.

Each of those minors had been interviewed, and each would be a witness at trial. And at least three of the minor males interviewed admitted that they had sent pictures of themselves posed in compression underwear to the defendant at the defendant's request. And, Your Honor, that would be-- that is a summary of the evidence substantiating the charged to which the defendant is pleading guilty, and that substantiates each element of the crime.

JUDGE: You admit admittedly the substance of your communications was the enticement to engage in a sexual act that would otherwise be a crime in Pennsylvania and perhaps elsewhere?

KANDEL: Yes, sir.
JUDGE: All right. Are you satisfied with that?
MS. OLSHEFSKI: Yes, Your Honor.
JUDGE: I am. All right. I'm going to ask you now, Mr. Kandel, how do you plead to the charge in count one in the indictment, guilty or not guilty?
KANDEL: Guilty.

Newswatch 16 at 5pm script from June 25, 2013:
A former educator from Lackawanna County stood in front of a federal judge today and pleaded guilty to online enticement of minors.

That judge accepted a plea deal to send Mark Kandel to prison for at least 13 years.

Mark Kandel of Peckville is a former educator and once sat on the Scranton school board. He was federally charged back in December on those child sex charges and today admitted to asking teenage boys to send him naked pictures on his phone and through Facebook.

Federal prosecutors charged Kandel with the online enticement of five teenage boys. They said Kandel sent thousands of text messages and Facebook messages to them that were sexual in nature and sometimes asked them for naked pictures.

At Kandel's guilty plea hearing at the Federal Courthouse in Wilkes-Barre, prosecutor Michelle Olshefski told a judge she could have charged Kandel with more child sex crimes... but instead they settled on a deal to send Kandel to prison for 13 to 19 years. Kandel pleaded guilty to one count of online enticement of minors.

In court, federal prosecutors went through the evidence they would have used if Kandel's case had gone to trial. Prosecutors say they spoke with 17 teenage boys who said they had sexual conversations with Kandel.

Prosecutors say three of those boys sent Kandel pictures of themselves in their underwear. Kandel is scheduled to be formally sentenced in September. He will also have to register as a sex offender as part of the plea agreement.

Newswatch 16 at 6pm script from June 25, 2013:
[Anchor: Scott]
A former Scranton school board director formally pleaded guilty today to online enticement of underage boys.

{pictures of Kandel here}

Mark Kandel appeared in federal court in Wilkes-Barre this morning to agree to a plea deal that would send him to prison for up to 19 years. These are pictures of him from a previous court date.

Federal prosecutors say Kandel sent thousands of text messages and Facebook messages to the boys that were sexual in nature and sometimes asked them for naked pictures. Kandel is scheduled to be sentenced in September.

The editorial decision at Newswatch 16 was made to exclude my name in these new reports because I had filed for divorce, and therefore, I was publicly acknowledging that I had cut ties with Mark. And I noticed articles in the newspapers also chose to omit my name. It was a relief to finally reach this point after months of cringing every time Mark's name was in the news. Luckily Mark's federal court appearance happened after Rachael and Sarah were out of school for the summer, allowing them to dodge any more embarrassment. The only hurdle left for them was Mark's sentencing, which was scheduled for some time in the fall.

■　　■　　■

The struggle to cover monthly financial obligations was getting more and more difficult. New contracts with WNEP contained slight pay increases, if there were any at all. I constantly worried about covering unforeseen expenses, the mortgage and home equity loan while still maintaining a lifestyle the girls were used to. I did not want to uproot them to move to a less expensive house because I wanted them to have the stability and comfort of staying in their home (and school district) while coming to terms with the fact that their dad was in jail. Refinancing the mortgage seemed to be the best option to take off some pressure. It took several weeks, but I collected all the necessary documentation and financial information needed for the bank to process the new loan only to get some very disappointing news from the loan officer.

"The only way the bank will refinance your mortgage is with Mark's name off the deed," he said. "Considering his circumstances, we can't have his name on the deed of the house if he can't be held financially accountable."

I almost fell to my knees, but the loan officer made perfect sense. How could someone in prison continue paying for the house if something were to happen to me?

And then, the thought crossed my mind that maybe, just maybe, I could convince Mark to sign off on the deed. I had no choice but to meet him in jail, something that turned out to be a lot more difficult than I ever imagined.

CHAPTER 23

The Lackawanna County Jail is located on a major street that connects downtown Scranton to the city's Green Ridge section. There is a popular corner bar across the street. A costume store, too. Single and multi-family homes all around it. During visiting hours, it would be hard to find parking on the street. When we lived in Green Ridge, I would drive by the jail a few times a day. Never did I think I would be someone searching for a parking space. Never did I dream I would be entering the jail for any reason other than it was related to a certain inmate or suspect who made the news.

But I wanted Mark to sign over the deed to the house so I could refinance the mortgage. So, I contacted the warden whom I knew through news stories. He was certainly aware of Mark's status at the prison. As it turned out, he became my next guardian angel. During regular visiting hours, you are not guaranteed to see your inmate. And I needed to know that I was going to see Mark.

The warden told me that because of my high-profile status, it would be less of a distraction if I visited Mark outside regular visiting hours and done privately. Call it special treatment, but I was not about to turn down his accommodations. The warden gave me a date and time and instructed me on what to do when I entered the lockup. No cell phones. No purses. Just identification which you give to the person at the reception desk for them to keep until you are checking out of the jail.

Even though I felt better about not having to sit in a waiting room full of strangers, I was petrified in the hours leading up to my visit. After all, I was still going to a jail. In all my years of reporting I had never done a jailhouse interview. And now, I was entering a lockup with the directions the warden gave me, but still not really knowing what to expect. What frightened me even more was the prospect of seeing Mark, face-to-face for the first time since I told him to leave the house in November. How would he look? What would he say? How much information do I share about the girls? Do I verbally attack him for the money he stole out of my annuity? All these questions raced through my mind.

With permission to leave the station for a few hours in the morning, I headed to the prison. Since it was outside of regular visiting hours, I found a parking spot on one of the side streets. The old part of the jail looks like a stone fortress. The public entrance is located in the newer part of the facility. I nervously walked in and gave the corrections officer behind the window at the check-in counter my cell phone and identification. He politely told me to take a seat in the waiting room, that someone would be with me shortly. Surrounded by grey-colored cinder block walls and sitting on cheap plastic waiting room chairs, I went over and over in my head what I would say to Mark. *You need to do the right thing and take your name off the deed to the house. Considering the circumstances, I had no choice but to divorce you. The girls are fine and let's leave it at that.*

In a matter of minutes, another corrections officer greeted and escorted me through a thick, metal door with electro-mechanical locks. It closed behind me, making a humming sound and then a thud. I was then led into a small meeting room with a round table and more plastic chairs. I was somewhat thankful I would not be talking with Mark through glass and over a phone like you see in the movies.

"He'll be here shortly," the corrections officer said. "Somebody is getting him now."

The officer then reminded me that he had to stay in the room for security reasons while Mark and I talked. The warden was doing me a huge favor by providing me with these special arrangements so having somebody else in the room did not bother me at all. If he overheard us talking about refinancing a mortgage, or any other private matters, then so be it.

Just then, a prison guard escorted Mark into the room. I caught my breath. His skin looked chalky-white, a stark difference from the tan glow he always had after the months of summer sun. It was obvious he had also lost some weight because his face looked thinner and his arms did not have the muscular tone they once had. He looked tired. By now Mark had been behind bars for six months. I assumed his physical changes had to do with the lack of sunshine and lousy, institutional food. The guards did not have him handcuffed, but he resembled a prisoner just the same, wearing a drab, olive green jumpsuit.

"How are you?" Mark asked as he instinctively embraced me, smiling as he always did. "And how are the girls?"

"The girls are surviving, as I am," I answered bluntly.

My answers during the few minutes of small talk were limited. *Why should he be privileged with information about our lives now,* I thought angrily.

There were so many things I wanted to ask him: Why did he carry on relationships with boys knowing he was breaking the law? Why did he lie to me again and again? Why did he go behind my back and take money out of my retirement accounts? But I did not want to overextend my welcome at the jail.

When I attempted to ask Mark about his upcoming sentencing in October, he offered no details except to say that friends and family were writing on his behalf in hopes the judge would be lenient. But he refused to offer any more information about his case or the possible punishment that faced him, insisting that "the walls have ears." So, we kept our conversation focused. I explained the dire financial strain I was under now and how important it was to refinance the mortgage, but in order to do that, he would have to agree to remove his name from the deed. I also reminded Mark that if the deed was still in his name and the feds imposed a significant fine as part of his sentence, a lien would be put on the home.

"And suppose any of the families of these teenagers in your case decide to file civil lawsuits?" I said to him. "As long as your name is still attached to the house, they can seize assets tied to our home."

Mark agreed to sign off on the deed and told me to return with all the necessary paperwork.

"You promise to cooperate in all this?" I asked. "You understand how crucial this is toward the welfare and future of your girls?" Mark nodded.

The corrections officer kept glancing at his watch. We both noticed and stood up.

"You know, I wish you could have come here to see me before you filed for divorce," Mark said as he was getting up from the table.

I felt the heat of embarrassment rising up my neck and onto my face. I could not look over at the officer. I could only imagine what he was thinking.

"What was I supposed to do?" I responded. "You are facing years in prison."

Mark continued, "But we could have worked something out without going through the divorce process."

I refused to respond to such utter nonsense. Was he really that stupid to think we could have 'worked something out' when he did what he did and was now facing up to 19 years in prison? *My God—he's fucking delusional,* I thought.

"I'll be back with the paperwork for you to sign," I said. Before I could pull away, Mark hugged me as he was escorted out of the meeting room. He never looked back at me as he was being led away, and I was quickly escorted out of the room by the corrections officer.

Never did I think I would be sitting in a room with a corrections officer and Mark in jail-issued clothing. How he hurt young boys, betrayed them, and ruined their lives. Never did I imagine my life would take such a sharp left turn. Never did I think I would be shouldering all the responsibility of a mortgage, expenses of raising two girls, car payments. But no matter how beaten down I felt, no matter how mortified I was visiting my soon-to-be-ex-husband in jail, I knew I had to somehow keep it all together for the sake of Rachael and Sarah.

I was married to a felon. I felt sick to my stomach. The whole thought of it pulled at me and my emotions snapped like a rubber band. How did this all happen? Every time I thought about it, which was practically all the time, I could feel the knot in my stomach tightening. I just wanted to wake up one day to find out that this was all a bad, bad dream.

■　■　■

I did not see Mark again until August.

This was the first summer that the girls did not have their father around. They tried to put on a good face for me but I knew, deep down, they were hurting. They were also hurting because for the first time in years, it looked as though we would not be taking our annual trip to Florida for summer vacation. Every summer the girls anxiously anticipated the road trip from Pennsylvania down the East Coast - staying overnight in Washington D.C., laughing at all the signs along Interstate 95 advertising the amusement park called *South of the Border* in South Carolina, and having a contest for the first person who spotted a palm tree. Those hours in our minivan laughing, talking, and playing travel games (travel bingo) were some of the most precious family moments. I longed for that again in the summer of 2013. But staying at the condo would trigger too many family memories for the girls and me.

Even though Florida was no longer an option, I still wanted to take the girls somewhere, anywhere, to help ease the pain. I felt they deserved time away after all the turmoil swirling around them the last several years. Leave it to David for suggesting the four of us take a trip to Maine.

After Mark was incarcerated, David took the girls under his wing while never overstepping any boundaries. He knew he could not replace their father, but he was there for important milestones like choral and band concerts, musicals, and high-school graduations. So, in the summer of 2013 he took the girls and me to one of his favorite vacation spots, Acadia National Park on Mount Desert Island in Maine.

It is a tradition for David's family to visit Bar Harbor every year. They started in the early 1970s and the trips continue to this day. David's family fell in love with Bar Harbor and Acadia National Park on Mount Desert Island because of its scenic beauty, peacefulness, and serenity.

Acadia is perfect for all kinds of outdoor activities like hiking, biking, kayaking, and camping. The view from the top of the majestic granite mountains is the best reward for making the climb.

In 1989, my parents and I went on a tour of New England – New Hampshire, Nantucket, Maine. We happened to be in Bar Harbor the same time as David's family, so he invited us to an outdoor lobster bake. It was one of the highlights of our trip. And that was the last time I had been in Bar Harbor. I was ready to go back.

The girls had never been to Maine so they were excited that this would be a whole new adventure. And by now, they were used to David being around. They understood how important he was in my life—not only as a colleague, but as a companion, friend, and handyman outside work hours. The girls knew David and I shared a special relationship long before I had met their father.

David thought by traveling somewhere new that was also a peaceful and quiet place would be a good distraction for the girls. David and his family had already reserved their week at a campground along Frenchman Bay for later that summer, but the opportunity to spend a second week in Maine with the girls and me thrilled him to no end.

He reserved the nicest and most expensive cottage at the campground for the end of July. And he made sure we had every accommodation possible. He even borrowed his nephew's four-door truck so we all could fit comfortably and still be able to haul all the recreational things we needed for the week including kayaks and gas grills. Soon after our journey began from Peckville early that morning, David shared something special with us that I will never forget.

"I wanted to find a theme song for our first trip to Maine together," he said. "And after much searching, I think I found it."

He reached over, pressed a button on the console, and Frank Sinatra's velvety voice reached out to us, but it was one of his songs we had never heard before – "Nothing but the Best," which Sinatra recorded in 1962 for his album *Sinatra and Swingin' Brass*. The song is about deserving only the best that life has to offer. David was always a big fan of Sinatra's music. And so was I.

As the upbeat, jazzy song played, I turned around to look at the girls. They both bounced to the rhythm of the tune. They were smiling. It melted my heart to see them so happy. For the first time in a long time, I saw the path to moving forward. Choosing this theme song was David's way of reassuring us that everything was going to be okay. It was his way of saying that the girls and I deserved only the best despite the horrible predicament Mark had put us in.

We spent the next 12 hours on the way to Maine talking and listening to music. I felt the stress knot start to come undone as we put more miles between us and Pennsylvania. When David turned into the Woodland Park campground outside of Bar Harbor, my stomach fluttered with excitement. Our home for the next week was a cottage called the Parrot, and it was nestled in large red oak and pine trees. The windows out back provided a gorgeous view of Frenchman Bay. The girls and I shared a cozy bedroom and bathroom with slanted ceilings on the second floor and David had the big bedroom on the first floor. We spent the week enjoying lobster bakes on the back porch, kayaking on the bay, hiking granite trails and biking around lakes and ponds in Acadia National Park.

Our week in Maine was far different from the vacations the girls were used to in Florida where we mostly just hung out by a pool or on the beach. In Maine, we spent most of our time surrounded by serene, natural beauty and our days were filled with activities. The girls loved it. The pristine Maine air washed away the ugliness that had been consuming our life back home. The ever-present knot in my stomach disappeared. For the first time, I felt like we were on the doorstep of a new beginning, that we could create a brand-new way of life. The trip was cathartic for me and certainly much needed considering I was facing another trip to the jail when we returned to Pennsylvania.

■   ■   ■

The idea seemed so simple at the time. Not long after I returned from Maine, I arranged for another visit at the Lackawanna County jail. I was told that a notary public worked on site and that they would be witness to the signature I was desperately after from Mark, but for some reason the notary was not available the day I visited. This was the improvised declaration I wanted Mark to sign:

To Whom It May Concern,

I, Mark Kandel, do voluntarily and without reservation state that I authorize that my name to be removed from the deed of the property at 5 Blythe Drive in Peckville, PA in order for Marisa Burke Kandel to immediately proceed with the necessary legal and financial actions to refinance the remaining mortgage on said property.

My decision to remove my name from the deed is based on the intention that this will allow Marisa Burke Kandel to reduce her monthly mortgage payments, so that she will be better able to pay all the upcoming higher education expenses for our daughters, Rachael Kandel and Sarah Kandel.

Let it be known that my top priority is the wellbeing and future education of my daughters Rachael and Sarah and I wholeheartedly decree that I wish that no legal issues or other complications deter them in the pursuit of their education, their ambitions or their dreams.

Mark Kandel

A few days later, my attorney received a fax from Mark's attorney.

"It has come to my attention that your client has attempted to have a document signed and notarized by my client, while he remains in the Lackawanna County Prison. Due to a notary being unavailable, this did not occur." Mark's attorney also made it clear he was not too thrilled with the meetings since we were in the midst of a divorce. My attorney emphasized that the visits with Mark were my idea and that he had no influence whatsoever.

"Such meetings between divorcing parties, outside of counsels' presence, have been occurring since the time of King Henry VIII and Catherine of Aragon," my attorney quipped.

Nonetheless, my attorney summoned me to his office where I showed him my homemade declaration that Mark had signed, but was not notarized. Since he signed the paper in the presence of a third party, a corrections officer, I thought the note would be sufficient.

My attorney looked at me as if to say, "you stupid fool." What he actually said was, "Marisa, if only it could be this easy, but we're talking about an official deed to a house."

He seemed skeptical right off the bat because nobody in their right mind would sign over the deed to a house if they were in the middle of a divorce and there was a disagreement over marital assets. Secondly, as an attorney he knew full well that I needed a professional to prepare and file the real estate transfer deed. Lastly, a notary must be present when a deed is signed over.

"So what if I withdrew the divorce petition?" I asked my attorney out of curiosity.

"Well, I guess that's an option if you feel more confident you can get all this achieved," he said.

"Then go ahead and inform Frank that we are withdrawing the petition. If the house is no longer an issue in a divorce, then there should be no problem for Mark to sign over the deed," I argued. It was not what I really wanted but I felt in the moment I had no choice. I was desperate to refinance the mortgage of our home so I could financially stay afloat.

My work schedule allowed for pockets of time during the day for me to deal with attorney appointments and jail visits. On September 6, I arranged for another visit with Mark. I told the warden it would not take that long. Again, we sat in the meeting room.

"If we both withdraw our petitions for divorce, then you can sign over the deed for me to refinance in hopes that we save the house," I told him. "Otherwise, I'll have no choice but to sell the house because I can't keep up with these monthly payments on my own."

Mark seemed pleased that I would no longer seek a divorce. His eyes had hope. A few days later I received a copy of a letter he sent to his attorney:

Dear Frank,

Marisa and I just met here at the Lackawanna County Prison and have decided to withdraw our petitions for divorce. We have decided to remain as a family. Hope all is well, and I look forward to seeing you soon.

Sincerely,
Mark

I paid a professional service to draw up a deed agreement that would relinquish Mark from the obligation and responsibility to the property and transfer full ownership to me. I sent Mark a letter telling him that I made arrangements with the jail to see him on October 3, 2013 for him to sign all the documents.

A woman who worked in traffic at WNEP was also a notary public and agreed to go with me. For the fourth time, I made arrangements with the jail to meet Mark in private. I felt by now I was becoming an annoyance because of the special arrangements made for each of our visits. I told the warden that "hopefully" this would be the last visit with Mark.

I was so hopeful and optimistic on my way to the jail. Once I got over this hurdle, I could take the necessary steps to refinance the mortgage and alleviate the financial stress I had been living with for months. When we entered the jail, a female corrections officer greeted us and told us to wait while another guard went to fetch Mark. Minutes later, she reappeared alone.

"I'm so sorry. He has a sign covering his jail cell window saying that he wasn't seeing anybody today," she said. "Did he know you were coming today?"

"Yes," I replied. "He definitely knew. We had exchanged letters. Do you mind trying to contact him again?"

"I will try," she said.

The corrections officer appeared a few minutes later and apologized again. "Nope. He isn't seeing any visitors today and as you know we can't force him to see anyone – not even his attorney," she said.

And then, I realized what probably happened. Mark's attorney probably interpreted my action to withdraw the divorce petition as a big tactic. Strategy. Manipulation. A game of chess, and I was looking for the *checkmate*. He probably went straight to Mark to say that the withdrawal was not sincere. That as soon as I got Mark's signature, I would reinstate the petition and continue with the divorce as planned. And then our home, probably worth close to $400,000 was no longer part of the divorce equation. I assumed he convinced Mark it was the wrong thing to do, so he weaseled out of our scheduled visit.

I never thought beyond getting Mark's signature. And now I was furious. After all this time, effort and money, I was nowhere closer to being in a better financial state to provide for my girls. I could not fathom how Mark could be so self-centered and put his own interests over the welfare of his two daughters! I wanted so badly to scream at him and tell him how much I hated him. I wanted to tell him how much of a selfish bastard he was, how his actions would negatively impact Rachael and Sarah.

I thanked the corrections officers and apologized for any inconvenience I had caused. I waited for the notary public to leave, and then got in my car and sobbed. This monster behind bars just complicated my life even more. I was so enraged about his latest stunt that I decided to head straight to his attorney's office across town.

The receptionist was a little taken back when I barreled into the office asking if I could see Frank. With no appointment. She left and a few moments later returned and directed me to his office. My heart was racing so fast I thought it would beat right out of my chest. Frank could see I was very upset, and the tension was stifling. It's highly unorthodox for a divorce attorney to have contact with his client's spouse. It just is not done. But my anguish and desperation left me no choice. I had to explain why it was important for Mark to sign over the deed to the house and for him to do the right thing.

"The girls have experienced so much upheaval in their lives because of what their father did, and I don't want to move them out of their home, just because I can't afford it anymore," I pleaded.

The last thing I wanted was to come across as some whimpering, weak, pitiful woman. I strongly stood my ground in front of him and made my case. Mark's attorney seemed sympathetic, but repeatedly mentioned how awful it was for Mark to be in jail. He told me he would talk with Mark but made no other commitments. I left that day feeling drained, distraught. I failed at what I had I set out to do that summer. I could only hope Mark would come to his senses before he was sentenced.

The day after I was supposed to see Mark my anger was still in intense, so I sat down and wrote him a letter. It was dated October 4, 2013. Here are a few excerpts from it:

By now you know I was at the jail today with the intentions of seeing you. Imagine my shock and disappointment when I was told you refused my visit. So after I left the jail I went directly to Frank's office. I've told you and Frank repeatedly that the bank will NOT complete the refinancing process until your name is off the deed. The reason for this is that you have no financial standing for several years to come while you are incarcerated. And the bank wants assurances that I and I alone will be responsible for the payment of the refinanced mortgage loan.

■　■　■

Despite what you may think or have heard, my motivations in all of this are NOT selfish. I could care less what happens to me. What I care about is the welfare and future well-being of Rachael and Sarah.

■　■　■

What did you think you would gain by not seeing me today? It was YOU who brought all this on by putting your personal desires before your family.

■　■　■

After the girls found out today that you refused to see me, they now both insist on writing letters to Judge Caputo asking for him to impose the maximum sentence on you.

Withdrawing the petition for divorce was off the table. I told my attorney to continue with the divorce. Full-throttle. After my visits to the jail that summer, I never saw Mark again. But he would continue to haunt me in ways I never imagined.

CHAPTER 24

You know when they say, "The hits just keep on coming." The phrase was originally used by disk jockeys when they played one popular record (hit) after another. So, sometimes, hits can mean one good thing after another is happening. But in a sarcastic way, the phrase means one negative thing after another is happening. A series of misfortunes.

Up to this point, I had experienced so many hits that I felt like an amateur fighter being pummeled by a professional welterweight boxer in the ring. Mark's first round with the law in 2008 was like a jab. A hook came at me in 2012. And now there was an uppercut waiting in my mailbox.

My daily routine included stopping at our mailbox after work. My stomach tightened when I noticed "IRS" in the return address. I have never known anyone to receive unexpected correspondence from the Department of Treasury that was good news. I certainly was not expecting this to be fan mail. My heart was beating faster as I opened the letter. My stomach tightened even more when I read it. Mark and I were being assessed a federal income tax liability of $16,717.00 for 2011, and $27,945.00 for 2012. Of course, the letter did not spell out why we owed the money, just that we owed. My hands were shaking. I was staring down the barrel of the IRS gun, and my suspicion was that Mark did something wrong, and yet again, did it behind my back.

My accountant was just as curious as I was, maybe even more, to find out what this was all about since he was the one who filed our taxes, so we headed to the IRS office in Scranton to find out. The receptionist recognized me and told me how much they enjoyed watching the news. A compliment, no doubt, but now these women were looking up my personal tax information to explain the IRS notice, and it all made me extremely uncomfortable. Again, I felt as though my privacy was being compromised.

We were given a detailed report that outlined the reasoning behind the assessment. I stood there in disbelief at what I was reading. But then again, after everything leading up to this, I guess I should not have been shocked.

In 2011, Mark withdrew over $35,000 from various savings accounts that were tied to Banker's Life and Casualty when he worked there. That $35,000 included the $13,798 from my annuity, some of his own annuities and retirement money. And he also emptied the girls' education savings accounts; money meant for their college education! He stole from his daughters and me. This was the money he was living on. And much of the money was either mine or intended for the girl's future. Again, I was flabbergasted at the extent of Mark's scheming ways.

The problem was, he never reported the income, and therefore, never paid the appropriate tax. Mark carried out the same scheme with other accounts in 2012. It was all very clear. Had Mark reported the income, he knew I would have found out about the money we would have owed the federal government when we compiled our taxes. So instead, Mark tried to hide the fact he drained all this money and the only way he could hide it was by not reporting the income.

My accountant and I surmised Mark did this for several reasons: he needed cash to pay for legal fees leftover from his 2008 legal troubles; he really did not have another job after he left Banker's even though he said he was working as an agent for New York Life; and he was looking for extra money to pay for all the items and gifts he was giving to those teenage boys. I now also understood how he was able to keep up with his portion of the mortgage payments and the home equity loan. After his father died in 2011, and accounts were dispersed among the surviving family members, he could no longer dip into those wells, so he turned to our savings and retirement accounts. Why an intelligent, well-educated man like Mark believed he could escape the Treasury Department by not paying taxes still boggles my mind today.

I didn't think my hatred for Mark could get worse, but this was that final punch. *Our children's education savings accounts.* His despicable behavior and deceit were limitless. I absolutely despised this man. And now, once again, I was left with a mess to clean up that I did not cause.

In the weeks that followed, my accountant spent hours corresponding with the IRS. He filed what is called an innocent spouse claim, basically arguing that I had no knowledge of, and should not have been responsible for, any tax liability of my now-estranged husband. I derived no economic benefit of the unreported income therefore, it was unfair to hold me responsible for the understatement of tax.

The time I spent trying to resolve this IRS issue was indeed nerve-racking, but thanks to the diligence of my accountant, the IRS granted the innocent spouse claim. I still had to pay several thousand dollars in taxes because of the way the IRS made some calculations on the money. I dipped into my savings account for that. But my accountant felt it was a small price to pay considering the original amount of the assessment.

The IRS fiasco again left me wondering how this man not only ruined his family by the crimes he committed but also nearly destroyed us financially. It was still difficult for me to fathom how this husband and father could betray us the way he did in so many painful ways. Justice would soon prevail because sentencing day was getting closer. My daughters and I were desperately seeking closure on all those years we were victimized by a liar and a cheat.

■　　■　　■

The mechanical issues plaguing Rachel's Audi were continuing, and the repair bills just kept piling up. Another connection to Mark that turned out to be a disaster. When another thousand-dollar repair estimate was handed to me in October 2013, I said, enough is enough. I could not justify paying $250 a month anymore on an unreliable car. It was time to get Rachael another car.

So, David and I headed to the Toyota dealership in Scranton where I always purchased or leased vehicles. My hope was to trade in the Audi and get a decent deal on a used car the girls could share. We spotted a Corolla that seemed perfect. Problem was, we still owed money on the Audi, and I could not afford paying off the Audi and buying another car at the same time.

Leave it to David to come up with a wise and brilliant solution.

"The outstanding loan for the Audi is still in Mark's name, correct?" asked David. "Leave the Audi here at the dealership. When the payments become delinquent, the bank won't come after you. They'll go after Mark, but he's in prison. So, the bank will repossess the car. But the repo won't affect your credit score whatsoever because the car was never in your name."

Bam!

Not only would this plan get rid of the Audi, I would get a bit of sweet revenge since the repo would affect Mark's credit score forever, not mine.

Two weeks later, there was a knock on my front door late at night. As much as it startled me, I answered. It was the repo company looking to tow away the Audi.

"It's parked at the Toyota dealership in Scranton," I said. "You can find it there." I shut the door, with a big smile on my face.

■   ■   ■

Mark faced 13 to 19 years in federal prison after pleading guilty to one count of online enticement of a minor. In the weeks leading up to his sentencing hearing, members of my family willingly sent letters to Judge Richard Caputo urging him to impose the maximum sentence. The following are the letters Rachael, Sarah, and I sent:

October 14, 2013
Dear Honorable Judge Caputo,

I am writing this letter to express to you how strong my feelings of betrayal are toward the man I once called my husband, Mark Kandel. I would love to say all of this in court the day Mark Kandel is sentenced. But because of my high-profile professional position, I do not want to turn your dignified courtroom into a media circus. Instead, please allow me to express my feelings through this letter.

This man who I once gave my unconditional love and trust to, put his own sexual desires toward innocent boys before his family. How any man could turn his back on his own wife and two daughters and put all that we've worked for in serious jeopardy for his own perverted gratification is completely beyond my belief and understanding.

But the fact remains. Mark Kandel has pleaded guilty to crimes against children. And as serious as that is, what is equally horrific is the betrayal and lying he committed to my daughters and me. I thought many times whether I should forgive him. And many times, since his incarceration a year ago, I've offered opportunities for Mark Kandel to show in his heart that he still cares for my daughters and me.

But despite my repeated efforts Mark Kandel has shown no intention of offering any type of future support financially or emotionally for his two daughters.

True, money isn't everything. But he has shown no effort to assume any responsibility at all for the future welfare of his daughters.

Perhaps what is most upsetting to my daughters and me is the fact that Mark Kandel has shown no remorse for the crimes he has committed. He sometimes talks about in letters he sends to us, that he is sorry for what he has put us through. But he has yet to say he is sorry for putting his own sexual desires with boys before his own family.

Your Honor, we have tried in our hearts to look for mercy. But in all honesty, we have found none, and ask you for none.

Back in 2008 when county charges were first brought against my husband, the girls and I stood behind him and gave him our unconditional support. But then in 2012 when federal prosecutors filed more serious charges against Mark Kandel, it opened our eyes to what type of man we had previously trusted and admired. And for the second time in four years my daughters and I had to endure public humiliation, embarrassment and ridicule.

Instead of being a loving, caring father, Mark Kandel is nothing more than a con man, a betrayer and a habitual child predator.

Because of this, my daughters and I have come to the decision that we absolutely do not want Mark Kandel to now, or ever be a part of our lives again. And because of this realization, I formally plead with you to sentence Mark Kandel to the maximum possible prison term allowed by law and that he spend that prison term as far away from our home in Peckville, PA as possible.

My daughters are terrified when they think of the possibility of once again going through the public pain and humiliation that they have experienced twice already when Mark Kandel is finally released from prison. The further in the future that you can make this happen, the better it will be for the welfare of my two teenage daughters who deserve to grow into adulthood without the weight of Mark Kandel's selfishness holding them back.

Respectfully,
Marisa Burke

October 14, 2013
Dear Honorable Judge Caputo,
I am writing in regards of my father Mark Kandel.
For the past 15 years of my life I held my father on a high pedestal. He was what I had thought to be the most sincere, loving and nurturing father. I thought we had an unbreakable bond like no other, and of course I was entitled, "Daddy's little Girl." Everything seemed right in the world when he was near, and I felt safe.

Things however took a turn for the worse a year ago when, for the second time, my father received charges involving the enticement of young boys. Imagine my shock as I discovered that the man who I above all admired the most had been living a double life no one else knew about. Not only have I experienced shock, I've felt betrayed, disgusted, mortified, and humiliated.

How can a man well off with a wonderful family throw everything he loved away for his own personal perverted desires? To go after innocent boys and to entice the very peers of his own two girls? Yes, this man who I am now ashamed to call my father went after my own friends and peers at the same school district where my sister and I are educated. Not only have I felt sympathetic to the boys and family members my father hurt, but I've also felt humiliated by the students who ridiculed my sister and me for my dad's crimes. My mom has also been ridiculed by complete stranger who we can only assume are viewers.

My father has left my mother alone to make the money, pay all the bills and run the house with no assistance. My mother is being bled dry of her finances and has told Rachael and me that she may not be able to support us to receive a college education. My sister and I both had planned on going to college, but now we don't know how we can afford it. My mom tries her hardest to provide for us, and is the most agonizing pain for us to watch her do it on her and feel so helpless.

I have seen the love my father had for us dissipate over the past year. Or perhaps the love was never there, after all it wouldn't be the first time he lied and kept things hidden. How can a man after ruining his family feel no remorse, or make no attempt to expiate for the hell he's put my family through? He is the epitome of selfishness and all other undesirable traits found in the soul of a malicious human being.

This is why I would suggest sentencing my father to the maximum punishment of more than 19 years in prison. It is not fair to these innocent boys, their families, my family, and all the other people involved and betrayed by my father to have him not do the time for his lawbreaking desires. Now only distance from and time away from my father will make me feel safe.

Thank you.

Sarah Kandel

October 14, 2013

Dear Judge Caputo,

I am writing this letter concerning my father, Mark Kandel.

For over sixteen years of my life I thought I knew a man who I admired beyond all reason. A man I trusted, a man who I thought could not have done one thing wrong, a man who I thought was going to be there for me the rest of my life guiding me toward the right paths and helping me make the right decisions. But this past year my life has changed, and the action that my father had made changed my mind on a lot of matters.

My father has been charged with sexual enticement of minors. It broke my heart that he would've done such a thing. This crime that he committed was so severe that it has to be taken in the matter of the federal system. This really opened up my mind so much. How could he have cared about those boys more than his own daughters? He even had the nerve to talk to these guys that attended the same school as me. Do you know how embarrassed we all were? A couple days after everything happened I couldn't go back to school because all the boys he texted were in my journalism class, and he was so oblivious to why I stayed home those two days. My father explains in his letters that he writes to my sister and me that he understands how hurt we are. He will never understand. He will never understand the betrayal he put us through and this is not the first time.

My father also did this to our family in 2008. We supported my father five years ago because that is what a family does, a family support system. But he did this a second time and if we supported him again he would've done it a third time and so on and so forth. How can we ever trust this man again? If he came back into our lives I could not believe one word he tells me. This man lied about everything.

Hypocrisy is one word that comes to mind when I think of my father. He always told Sarah and me to be good Christians and to attend church every Sunday when he would turn right around and make fun of someone. He even hurt his own family and he's telling us to be good Christians? It just does not make sense to me. My father made fun of everyone who was there ready to help my mother, my sister, and me after everything happened. He shot everyone down, and for what? Where did this ridicule of others get him?

Toward the very end, I felt lost. My father would not even pick his head up to say hello to Sarah and me. Instead he would be on Facebook messaging these young boys or texting them. There was never one moment where he wasn't on his phone. He would pay more attention to his phone than to me. And as a child I seek attention from my parents and I just wasn't getting that from my father. I tend to wonder if my father even feels bad that he is missing out on so many upcoming events in my life, like me being "Dolly" in "Hello Dolly" in my high school's musical this year, or me walking down to receive my diploma this year, or me walking down the aisle at my wedding, or even the opportunity to meet grandkids. My father had a great life and he just threw it all away, and for what?

This has all been bottled up inside of me for the past year and it took a while to get it all on paper. If my father had just taken the necessary steps in signing over everything to my mother, I wouldn't have had to write this letter. That just shows my father's true colors too. If he really cared about my sister and me, he would've signed everything over so my mom could refinance our house and we could have more financial assistance for college and now college next fall isn't looking so clear for me or for Sarah.

My mom is my hero and I admire her so much after the year she's had as well. My father left and resulting from that dumped everything on my mother. I have never seen my mother so bombarded with bills and mortgage payments now that my father has left us. We are helpless financially now and we are unsure about what the future has in store for us.

I'm letting everyone know right here and right now that I am seventeen years old, I'm almost an adult and I have a mind of my own. No one influenced me to write this letter, no one influenced me to visit or not to visit my father in jail, and no one influenced me about attending my father's sentencing. You Judge Caputo and everyone out here today have to realize how hurt I am. Imagine someone you loved and admired your life disappearing with no remorse. How would that make you feel? Lastly, I did want to attend this sentencing today and read the letter myself. But my father does not deserve my presence and he will not see me ever again and I don't want to see him ever again. I apologize to everyone who my father hurt and betrayed and maybe you all feel the same as I do. Unfortunately, it took all of this for me to realize everything that this man has done to us.

Thank you for taking the time to read my letter.

Rachael Kandel

Assistant U.S. Attorney Michelle Olshefski tried to persuade me to go to court the day Mark was sentenced to help send a message that we all wanted the maximum punishment of 19 years. But I just could not commit because, as I stated in my letter to Judge Caputo, I did not think it would be fair to turn the judge's courtroom into a media circus. Being a news personality and local celebrity, much of the press attention would have been on me and capturing my reaction to what was going on in court. Rachael had no interest in going to court either and instead went to school.

But Sarah insisted on being there to read the letter she had she sent to the judge. A close friend of mine took her to federal court in Wilkes-Barre and remained in the courtroom until she was finished with her testimony. It took a tremendous amount of strength and courage for this 16-year-old to stand up in front of her father and passionately convey her feelings about this man she once called, "the best daddy in the world." She told me later that her father showed no emotion as she read her letter.

Sarah and the 17-year-old victim mentioned in the federal indictment were the only two who testified for the prosecution that day. Mark's brother and a minister from Mark's church testified on his behalf.

After that, the judge addressed Mark before he handed down his sentence. This is the transcript I obtained from federal court:

JUDGE: "All right. Well, one of the things that's evident is how the situation has torn your family apart. I don't think I need to comment any more about that. I mean, it's evident, and I would hope that, on reflection, you'll find some way to reconcile that. But that is what these kinds of things do to people, this is what these kinds of things do to families, and it's understandable.

The factors I have to consider in arriving at an appropriate sentence here in a range that's been agreed to, by the factors in Title 18, 3553(a), the first of which is the nature and circumstances of the offense.

I don't want to engage in characterizing this offense, we know what it is, we know that it's a reflection of a depraved situation, and we know that it's not acceptable in civilized society. There is no legitimate excuse. There may be a medical or psychological excuse about which I'm not familiar, but there is no excuse. The fallout from this sort of thing, as evidenced by the young man who testified here today, is also something that tells us why it's a bad thing, it tells us why it's not acceptable in civilized society.

But I'm not going to lecture you, because you're an educated person, and you know that, without question. Whatever the demons are that you have, I presume you'll address them. I don't know how you will do that, but I know that you will address them, at least, if you care to go the way you say you want to go.

So this is a very serious offense. I've had a number of these similar, dissimilar involving the same sort of thing. It's just not acceptable in our world.

Your personal history and characteristics. Mixed, frankly, because you had difficulty like this in the past. You say, okay, well, balance that with all the good that I've done. All of the good that one has done in one's life never is enough payment for one bad act. It never fails. Every time we have a sentencing, we hear about all the good that someone has done, which is fine, and their life should be characterized before a sentencing judge, I agree with that. But it never can compensate for the bad. It just never can overcome the bad.

There is no question you've bettered yourself, in terms of education. You've devoted yourself to education. You've always worked. You've been a responsible individual. But that's what we're supposed to do. We don't want to pat ourselves on the back for doing what we ought to do, especially, if you have talent, and you have talent.

I have – a little child once said a very profound thing. He said, we're busy because we have ability. You were productive because you have ability, which is to be expected.

But nevertheless, it has been your life, and you had a good life and you had good family life until this event.

Your brother's remarks speak of family feeling that not many people have, certainly, people who have appeared in front of me.

As on the other hand, your daughter has indicated the terrible betrayal that she feels and your family feels, as a result of your conduct, which, by the way, is really what is so serious about this offense.

Your position as a mentor to these young people, having their trust, and then betraying it. And it's really what makes this, also doubly difficult and doubly bad, really. It's the whole situation where the mentor takes advantage of the person who holds the mentor in awe. It's a very easy mark, and you took advantage of these easy marks.

On the other hand, to some extent, they were 16, 17 years old they also got to the point where, maybe, they should have known better, too, but nevertheless, the law still protects them, so we have to think about that.

So in any event, I think that's pretty much a characterization of the nature and circumstances of the offense and your personal history and characteristics.

The need for the sentence that I impose has to reflect the seriousness of the offense, promote respect for the law and provide just punishment. I will do that.

To afford an adequate deterrent, that is to say, to discourage anybody else from doing the same or similar thing. This is the so-called message aspect of a sentence to send the message out into society that, if you do this, here's what's going to happen to you.

To protect the public from further crimes by you. I have to take that into account because there is a history here.

To provide you with any needed educational or vocational training, medical care or other correctional treatment. I don't consider that to be a factor that needs to be weighted very heavily because of your obvious educational background and your accomplishments in education.

The need to avoid unwarranted sentencing differences among defendants who have similar records and who have been found guilty of similar conduct. I do have some experience in that area, with respect to the behavior that's in this general field, maybe, not exactly the same but close enough.

So all these thing considered, and in looking at the range of sentence, it's my view that an appropriate sentence in the case is 174 months. That's the sentence I'm going to impose."

For those of you doing math, the sentence amounted to 14 and a half years in prison. Naturally, Mark's sentencing on October 28, 2013 was the big story of the day. Many of the news stories on air, online, and in the newspapers mentioned Sarah's testimony against her father and the testimony from the 17-year-old victim in the case. While I was able to stay on air when Newswatch 16 reported on his plea, I knew I would not be able to do any fancy maneuvering of the order of stories for a story this big. So, I was excused from work. But, thankfully, it would be the last time.

Before Rachael got home from school and Sarah came home from court, I spent my day catching up on household chores, walking the dog, and exercising. I refused to look online or watch any reports on the noon news. And it was not until my friend who took Sarah to court called me that I learned of Mark's sentence.

This was one of several stories that ran on Newswatch 16 that evening:

[ANCHOR]

A former educator from Lackawanna County will start serving a federal prison sentence for sending students he mentored lewd text messages.

Mark Kandel was sentenced today to 14 and a half years behind bars.

{pictures of Kandel here}

Mark Kandel is a former Scranton school director and a longtime employee of the Northeastern Educational Intermediate Unit #19 in Archbald. He was arrested almost a year ago for sending sexual text messages to five teenage boys.

It was last November when the Lackawanna County DA's office arrested former educator Mark Kandel of Peckville. Two teenage boys had come forward saying Kandel sent them sexual text message. Then, federal investigators got involved. Eventually charging him with the online enticement of five teenage boys.

Kandel faced 50 years in prison but a federal judge accepted a plea deal to sentence him on only one charge of online enticement.

A courtroom full of people heard from one of his victims, a young man who received text messages from Kandel when he was a student at Valley View High School. The victim said he and other boys were promised money in exchange for their communication. The victim said he was ridiculed by other students after he came forward.

There's no parole in the federal system, so Mark Kandel will spend the next 14 and a half years behind bars. And another part of his sentence, Kandel will have to register as a sex offender for the rest of his life.

Neither the girls nor I had the slightest curiosity or intention to watch the news that night. We instead accepted an offer by some very close friends to join them for dinner at a fine restaurant. And of course, we all took part in a celebratory toast – not because Mark was going to prison for a long time, but for the girls and I finally closing a very dark, very long chapter in our lives and forging ahead as stronger individuals and a new family unit – just the three of us.

CHAPTER 25

Mark Kandel: Prisoner Federal Prisoner 70917-067

Mark was taken from the Lackawanna County Prison where he was held until sentencing and transferred to The Federal Correctional Institution in Fort Dix, New Jersey, which is a low-security prison for male inmates. In a letter he sent to Rachael in December, Mark described how there were 12 men to a room, six bunk beds with a small table and locker for each person. He mentioned that he was successful in getting a tutoring position in the prison's education department. He also wrote:

I'm not angry with you or Sarah for writing the Judge. I know these are things you needed to say. I just wish you two would have come to the prison last year and told me face to face. I think about you every moment and pray daily that God watches over you and gives you the strength to get through these difficult days. Time does heal. I can never say "sorry" enough for the pain and hurt I caused you all.

My hope and prayer is that time will heal and when I leave here in 2025, I will be able to re-establish a relationship with both of you.

Mark continued writing to the girls for a few months and then the letters stopped. I assumed because the girls refused to write back. They had nothing to say to him. And I understood that.

While Mark's criminal case was closed, the divorce proceedings were ramping up, and it appeared Mark's attorney was digging in his heels for a fight. The first one came as David and I started selling Mark's sports memorabilia on eBay. All that stuff in our basement, remnants of Mark, haunted me. I wanted it completely out of our home. And, it was a way to make some extra cash.

David helped me put the items on eBay because he was much more computer savvy than I. A Brett Favre autographed football fetched $73. Autographed Pittsburgh Penguins Sidney Crosby framed jersey? $365. An autographed Larry Csonka replica Miami Dolphins helmet sold for $90. We managed to sell 33 items for a profit of $766.94 when our online operation was abruptly shut down.

"By any chance, are you selling Mark's sports items on eBay?" asked my divorce attorney. "Mark's attorney is questioning the whereabouts of certain items of personal property and stresses that these items were of sentimental value to his client."

Bullshit, I thought. I was convinced that Mark used those items to entice young guys into our basement and to impress them with his collection. My mind then went to our pool. I believe he talked those young guys into coming over for a swim so he could get off watching them frolic in the water with their shirts off. At first, I denied I was selling any items online. Maybe it was because my defenses immediately went up. After more questioning by my divorce attorney, I felt I had no choice but to fess up.

Turned out someone anonymously tipped off Mark's attorney that we were selling his sports valuables online. Problem was, all these items were considered part of the marital assets and should not have been touched. I could only conclude that it was a man who used to work with Mark at Banker's and who connected Mark with Frank. He stopped over one night to see how the girls and I were doing, and I told him that I was starting to sell Mark's sports memorabilia online. After that evening, I never heard from or saw him again.

Mark's divorce attorney must have thought we had sold tens of thousands of dollars in sports collectibles, and therefore needed to put that back in the pot for equitable distribution. Before one of many divorce hearings, David was subpoenaed to testify in court and produce documents for what he had sold on eBay. But when he showed Mark's attorney that we sold only seven-hundred dollars' worth of stuff, Frank backed off and never mentioned the collectibles again. Looking back now, all of those items should have been part of the marital assets, but Mark wanted them all back, and Greg and I ended up making the concession.

Even so, the bickering over the rest of the marital assets continued and our divorce case led to many hearings before a Lackawanna County Family Court judge. Mark was supposed to "attend" some of them via phone. But every time the court tried to make the connection we were told there was 'some sort of problem' at Fort Dix.

Mark's attorney was going through every single marital asset with a fine-tooth comb, from the value of our home to the value of my retirement accounts. Correspondence and arguments between our lawyers were non-stop. Sarcastic emails were traded. Phone calls were heated. And personalities clashed. Especially in court. Greg was low-key and soft-spoken but attacked like a snake at the appropriate moments. Mark's attorney, Frank, was loud and aggressive.

Through it all, Greg remained optimistic, but we both knew I stood to lose a lot of money because I was the prime breadwinner for our entire married life. And that is what aggravated me more than anything else. Considering how that man destroyed his family with betrayal, lies, deceit, theft, and scandal and nearly blew up my career, I did not think Mark deserved a flipping dime!

What turned out to be the last hearing before Judge Patricia Corbett took place in October of 2014. Greg and I had a feeling the judge would rule on a divorce settlement, but we were not entirely sure. We sat down at one table while Frank and his legal assistant were at the table on the opposite side of the courtroom. A few yards in front of us sat the judge. Just like you see on TV.

The attorneys immediately began arguing for their respective sides. I thought, *here we go again. Nothing will be accomplished again today.* Both sides agreed that I would be responsible for the house since Mark would be incarcerated for the next 14 and a half years. And as soon as the deed was solely in my name I could - finally – proceed with refinancing the house. But the argument was over the split of marital assets. Would it be 30/70, 40/60, 50-50 and in whose favor? I heard about nightmares like this from others who suffered through messy divorces. Never in my wildest dreams did I think I would be going through the same kind of torture—especially when my husband was behind bars!

Mark's incarceration did not matter to his attorney. According to him, since we had been married for 20 years, Mark deserved a cut of the pie. And a BIG one. Frank laid out his case as to why the settlement should be at least 40/60 in favor of his client. There was more yelling. More screaming. Judge Corbett summoned both attorneys to her chambers. I sat there thinking—*this is it, I'm doomed.*

When they came back into the courtroom, the attorneys picked back up where they had left off. Then, unexpectedly, Judge Corbett said, "Obviously, it is impossible to hear what the defendant in this matter has to say because he is incarcerated. But Marisa, is there anything you would like to say?"

The courtroom was tense. Both attorneys were standing as they made their arguments, so I got up and stood next to Greg. I thought, *this is my make or break it time, Marisa. Say what you want to say or forever hold your peace.*

"Your honor, if I may address the court for just a few moments. First, I want to say that I never thought I would be in divorce court. I never wanted a divorce. I married Mark 20 years ago thinking we were going to have the perfect life together. We had two beautiful daughters together. We both had excellent careers. Things were going so well. But after he broke the law, I had no choice but to file for a divorce. My employer, WNEP-TV wanted proof that I was breaking ties with this guy, otherwise, I truly believe my long and prosperous career would have been in jeopardy. And had I lost my job, how would I have provided for my two children since their father is now locked up?"

My voice started quivering. "Your honor, our family has been put through hell. Since 2008, my daughters and I have been forced to live under a cloud of embarrassment, humiliation, and shame all because his (pointing to Mark's attorney) client broke the law, lived a double life, and lied to his family. I did not ask for this and I certainly do not want to be in this courtroom. But I had no choice, your honor. No choice. I am here to hopefully salvage what I can so I can continue providing a decent life for my girls who deserve only the best."

There was silence for a few moments. Frank and Greg looked at the judge waiting for her to make the next move. I sat back down in my seat and wiped away tears.

Then Judge Corbett said, "I have made my decision. I am ruling 75/25—in Marisa's favor."

Greg and I showed no emotion. But I was exploding inside! I finally achieved victory after years of tumult and heartache. Frank and his legal assistant looked deflated as they packed up their briefcases. Before Frank left, he turned to me and wished me good luck. I felt hatred toward him throughout the divorce process but admired him for having the gusto to fight for Mark. He was just doing the job he was hired to do.

Before Judge Corbett excused herself, she came down off the bench, walked over to me, and gave me a big hug. She asked if I was doing okay. I just shrugged my shoulders and thanked her for being so thoughtful.

"It's time to get on with your life," she whispered in my ear before she turned around and left.

Greg and I waited until we were out of the courtroom and outside on the sidewalk to express how we both felt. "I've been a divorce attorney for a long time," he said. "And I never had a 75/25 ruling from a judge. Never. And Marisa, both you and I know it should have been in Mark's favor because you were the money maker all these years. But the judge turned it right around in your favor. My God!"

I did have to cash in one of my retirement accounts to the tune of $105,000 to settle the divorce. But my other retirement accounts were safe, and I got the house.

On December 15, 2014 the President Judge of Lackawanna County signed our divorce decree, and my life with Mark was legally and officially over.

■　　■　　■

As much as I had wanted to succeed in broadcast journalism, I also had dreamed of a picture-perfect personal life – the American dream. To me, it was following in my mother's footsteps: getting married, buying a home, having children. I knew that having a family with sound, moral values would also cement my standing with viewers. So, while I was working hard to build my career, I was also looking to find a man, fall in love, get married, and start a family.

There I was already in my 30s. Dating a few guys, but no one special. A few trysts here and there. I heard my biological clock. It was ticking loud and in sync with my heartbeat. I knew if I wanted to have a family, something better happen and soon.

That's when I met Mark.

A wonderful sense of humor, intelligent, kind, caring, charming and genuine.

Take note to that last description. Genuine.

Back then, I believed that Mark was the real deal. I could see him as a wonderful partner, a thoughtful father. He would also be the perfect husband to solidify my professional image. The magic of WNEP-TV's success was making viewers' families feel they were part of the families of the on-air personalities. The more you could share about your private life, the more you could relate to your audience so that they would tune in day after day. I wanted to be a good employee and wanted to have the idyllic family life to share with my audience.

So, I shared. My wedding day. The first few hours of my daughters' lives in a hospital room. Mark and me attending charity events and civic engagements.

The way our happy life was portrayed to our viewers was the way I really wanted it to be. Of course, when Mark and I stood at the altar, I had hoped we would love and respect each other forever. I had hoped we would have a long-lasting marriage brimming with passion. I had hoped we would build and maintain a freeway of two-way communication. Just like all the other happy couples I knew and read about.

But our relationship ended up being more like a business, a partnership. We were a couple, but much like salt is to pepper. The further we got from our wedding day, the more our relationship turned into a friendship. We were not lovers or people madly in love. And even though I sensed there was something not right between us, I allowed it to happen. I allowed our household to continue with traditional roles of husband and wife, father and mother because it helped enhance my career.

The problem was Mark and I never built that two-way highway of communication. We avoided talking about our feelings. As we settled into daily life of family, jobs, busy schedules filled with commitments, it was just easier to avoid controversy than address what was lacking in our marriage. The loss of intimacy was accepted and tolerated. But now I know that should have been a huge warning sign.

I have heard it said that there must be truth in order to have trust. Our marriage was one of convenience and compatibility but in the end, lacked emotional truthfulness. Yes, Mark was not truthful with me. But I should have been more truthful with myself. Looking back, much of my marriage was untruthful because I refused to see what I did not want to see. Perhaps, that is the reason I shrugged off the changes in Mark's behavior, the growing infatuation he had for his phone, the gradual lack of interest in sex and excuses he made for crawling into bed at 3 o'clock in the morning. Clues that Mark was attracted to young men may have been in plain sight. His collection of Abercrombie and Fitch catalogues. The young men he "mentored and tutored." The pool parties reported by strangers that may have occurred behind my back, and basement hang-outs. The mysterious disappearance of his personal laptop after our trip to Michigan. The jaunts he took to East Stroudsburg and Shippensburg to attend fraternity parties. Our sexual relationship fading away. All the years of both of us using the "too busy" and "too tired" excuses.

Despite all these warning signs, I refused to admit that I married a man who could not come to terms with his sexuality. I chose to carry on the charade our marriage *was* rather than recognize and admit what it *was not*. All to save face. Until 2008, no one outside our home knew or questioned what our private dynamic was like. My television audience perceived that I was living the ideal family life.

Then everything came crashing down again in 2012. Mark's criminal behavior was bad enough because it exposed who he truly was. But it also cast suspicions on our private life. In a way, the charade of our marriage was also exposed. The man I happily married became the subject of news stories, and suddenly our wholesome family image was tarnished among my viewers. That is what made the public humiliation so much more agonizing. And for the first time ever, I did not want to be me.

My refusal to open my eyes to the realities of my marriage and who my husband was, however, does not mean I knew about his criminal behavior and turned a blind eye to it. I want to set the record straight on this because some people thought I somehow knew about Mark's inappropriate behavior with those teens yet did nothing about it. "How could she not have known?" I heard time and time again.

Very simple. Mark led a double life. He was a con artist. I never thought that the fun-loving, devoted husband and father I knew could evolve into a self-centered, deceiving, narcissistic individual capable of crimes against children. This was not the man I married. This was not the man I thought I knew. I wish I had given more credence to the warning signs. I wish Mark could have been open and honest with me about his sexuality. I wish my vision had been 20/20 in 2008 rather than in hindsight…

Whenever I look back on the events of my life, I now question the path I chose and the choices I made. How many red flags did I miss or dismiss for the sake of preserving an angelic image both professionally and personally? In the end, I tolerated my marriage being a sham. Mark did too. But pretending only goes so far. It landed Mark in prison for a long time. It upended my life in ways I never could have imagined.

That's why my move out of Peckville in the summer of 2015 was cathartic and symbolic. After the divorce, I was finally able to refinance the mortgage when the deed was solely in my name. But by then, the girls were going off to college, and I could not wrap my head around being in that huge house by myself. So, two years after Mark went to federal prison, I decided it was time to move into a smaller home and I searched for one all over the Lackawanna Valley. But nothing seemed like the right fit. So, I started looking beyond "the valley" and that's when a listing caught my eye. The home was located—on top of a mountain. The quaint and quiet bedroom community I found about 25 miles from Scranton was appropriately called Mountain Top.

The home had just been built, never been lived in and was about half the size of our home in Peckville. It was surrounded by woods. The property was private and isolated. It felt like the perfect place to heal.

A mountain can symbolize climbing out of despair, overcoming obstacles, and making progress. Rising above turmoil and improving yourself. I realized I had been living in a valley of despair, figuratively and literally. I wanted to reclaim my dignity and begin the process of self-forgiveness. While my life was forever changed by Mark's actions, I was ready to move forward to build a new life. And Mountain Top seemed like a good place to start.

It has been said that humiliation, a "public emotion" is worse than death. It destroys how people perceive us. And when we are humiliated by someone we love, the disappointment and despair is even more agonizing. It can spark anger, revenge, and deep pain.

My closest friends told me had they been in my shoes, you would have found them in a fetal position in the corner of a padded room. Initially, I chuckled at such comments. But then I think of just how close I was to "losing it." My reputation as a wife was ridiculed and questioned. My reputation as a television personality was nearly ruined. I worried about what my peers and supervisors thought, whether I would lose my job. I was the victim of gossip. It would have been much easier for me to just give up. But I could not. I had two girls who needed me.

In early August of 2015 the movers came and trucked all our belongings to Mountain Top. Our home in Peckville was now completely empty. Even though the afternoon sun pierced through the front windows, the home seemed lifeless and sad. It was time for one last walk-through. Rachael, Sarah, and me. Together we walked into their bedrooms. I remembered rocking Sarah at bedtime as I gave her the last milk bottle of the day. And Rachael loved when Friday rolled around because the "Friday fairy" (me) would make her bed in the morning. We talked about the times both girls would sneak into each other's bedrooms across the hall after they thought their father and I were asleep and would not hear them. The three of us smiled.

We made our way downstairs and looked around our family room – the gathering place for so many birthday parties, lots of family traditions, and wonderful holiday gatherings. I could almost feel the glow of the fireplace that had kept us cozy through many long winters. I could see our beautiful Christmas tree in the place it stood year after year and how the windowpanes of the French doors reflected the colored mini-twinkle lights on the tree.

We ended our walk-through standing in the kitchen, the heart and soul of our home. The countless meals and discussions around the dinner table were always special times for us.

When we moved to Peckville 17 years ago, Rachael was two and Sarah was just a little more than a year old. So, I witnessed them going from babies to toddlers to grade-schoolers and finally teenagers. My girls had matured into fine young women, and I truly believe that the comfort, security and stability of our home contributed to their successful upbringing. That is why I had been so determined not to move in the midst of Mark's criminal trouble.

"Goodbye home, you served us well," I said out loud with tears in my eyes. "I wanted to believe the good memories outweighed the bad." The girls nodded in agreement.

With that, I placed the house keys on the kitchen counter for the new owners and shut the door behind us. I watched the girls get into Rachael's car and drive away from the neighborhood. As I pulled out of the driveway, I stopped and glanced back at our house one more time. I felt nostalgic for the happier times.

I felt sad for the bad times. I felt ready to focus on looking out the windshield rather than in the rear-view mirror.

As I drove slowly away from the house and toward the entrance of the development, a swirl of emotion enveloped me. I wondered what was next after years of torment and emotional torture.

I have learned so many lessons since 2008. Some family and friends will walk through your lowest point with you while others will distance themselves. Losing some of the people in my life broke my heart. But even though my circle is now much smaller, I know I can trust each person in it.

I now listen to my gut reactions because intuition energizes judgment. I no longer second-guess my suspicions, but act on them. I will never ignore or not act just for the sake of saving face or protecting the illusion of an "ideal life."

Letting go of the past and all that happened is difficult for me. I do not believe I will ever understand why Mark led a double life. As much as I want closure, and to leave it all behind me, I think it will be next to impossible because I never got to say final words to him, and probably never will.

Even so, I will not give in to self-pity. I despise that I had to experience all this, but sinking into the quicksand of self-pity does nothing for my mental and physical health.

I'm not sure I can forgive and forget. Again, I'm okay with that.

I have stopped trying to be the same person I was before all this happened because I am not. The heartbreak, shame and humiliation have changed me, have scarred me forever. There is no Band-Aid® big enough to fix that. It is a deep wound that will never completely heal.

My recovery is ongoing. I have done much soul-searching and self-reflection. I want to believe I went from victim to victor. But the only way to do that, is to realize that Mark's shame is not my shame.

EPILOGUE

Proms. Plays. College visits and acceptance letters. Performing arts school. High school and college graduations. First jobs. Turning 18. Turning 21. Moving to new states. Making big, grown-up decisions. Mark has missed, and will continue to miss, so many milestones in his daughters' lives.

Despite all the turmoil and humiliation the girls endured throughout their middle school and high school years, they not only graduated, but did so with honors. Both landed either prominent or lead roles in all of Valley View's musicals during their four years. And Rachael was chosen to sing at her high school graduation in 2014. The song she sang was an appropriate song for that moment in time: "For Good" from *Wicked*.

Valley View helped nurture the passion both Rachael and Sarah acquired for drama, theatre and music. And after high school graduation, Sarah trained in musical theatre at the American Musical and Dramatic Academy in New York City and graduated in February of 2017. Rachael spent her second-to-last semester studying overseas in The Netherlands. She graduated from East Stroudsburg University in May of 2018 with a degree in Hospitality, Recreation and Tourism Management. She caught the travel bug visiting different countries, and it is her dream to see all seven continents.

The girls do not want to visit their father. They never want to see or talk to him again. A few months after we moved to Mountain Top, they legally changed their last name from Kandel to Burke. We had to go before a Luzerne County judge who ruled on the name change and coincidentally -- the judge's last name just happened to be Burke.

I am proud that Rachael and Sarah moved beyond this nightmare. Federal prosecutor Michelle Olshefski said, "they were totally traumatized, totally affected by his conduct. Their lives have been irreparably damaged and forever changed." But my girls persevered. They are self-motivated, energetic and ambitious young women who dream big and think positively.

I would like to think that their successes in life so far are a testament to the way I raised and protected them after Mark was no longer part of our lives. Being thrust into the role of single parent was not in my original life blueprint, but I did the best I could. I appreciate any man or woman who assumes that role and responsibility of being both the mother and father, the only disciplinarian, the counselor, the psychologist, and the sole breadwinner.

I did not jump into dating after my divorce, but instead put all my energy into helping the girls navigate college life and early adulthood. David has remained a very close friend, but there has been nothing romantic in my life for quite some time. I question whether I will ever be able to trust a man enough to totally let him into my life and heart.

A geographic move helped my emotional recovery. I had been a life-long Pennsylvania resident, but Colorado was the oasis that my heart needed. I fell in love with the Centennial State after visiting my brother in 2016 and moved there two years later.

The only thing that was stable throughout those years after Mark's incarceration was my job. But that too came to an end in October 2016 when WNEP's parent company, Tribune Media, offered a buyout to several employees with 30 or more years' experience. I fell into that category. While management made it very clear that I was not being forced to leave, after nearly 33 years at the same station, I was ready. Personally and professionally, it was time to move on.

So, on October 28, 2016, I said farewell to my audience one last time. Words cannot express how appreciative I am to WNEP-TV for keeping me employed for more than three decades and for having faith in me despite Mark's legal issues. Soon after I retired from broadcast journalism, I started my own multi-media agency. And started writing this book.

I hope my story empowers and encourages other women to immediately wave the red flags when something seems suspicious, have the courage to do what is right even though it may rock the family boat, be strong enough to trust your instincts, and to act on those instincts with fortitude and without fear.

ACKNOWLEDGMENTS

I wrote the first draft of this book in 2016 shortly after I accepted a buyout from WNEP-TV. Reliving the story broke my heart all over again, but if sharing it helps even just one woman, the heartache will be well worth it.

Many people encouraged me to write the book, including Michelle Olshefski, the federal prosecutor assigned to Mark's case. And not because it would shine a spotlight on the case or her victory in it. But because she felt that it could benefit many women who may someday find themselves in a similar situation.

I have tremendous gratitude to my closest girlfriends. Above all, Jackie Frank. She was my rock in the midst of my turmoil. She cried with me, consoled me, and held my hand when I needed it most. I always say that Jackie is the sister I never had.

I am so glad my late father did not witness what happened to me in 2008 and 2012. He would have been heartbroken. Unfortunately, my mother did. And like me, I am sure she felt waves of embarrassment, shame, and humiliation each time she saw news reports about her son-in-law. While both of my brothers lived in other parts of the country, I know they were very concerned about my welfare and that of the girls during those tumultuous times. I thank them and my mother for being so protective of me and for offering their never-ending support.

This book would not have been possible had it not been for my closest friend, David Krisanda. He not only pulled me from the darkest depths of despair, but he has been my confidant and conscience during the high and low points. He has, and always will be, my voice of reason. He understands me better than anybody else in the world. I only hope we can grow old knowing that we will always be there for each other no matter what life turns out to be.

I thank Dawn Leas for being the creative genius in helping to write and edit this book. We bonded as soon as I met her in November of 2019. Being a published poet and experienced teacher, she helped guide me during the final phases of this project with intelligence, dignity, and honesty.

I will be forever grateful to my WNEP-TV family. Looking back at those devastating years, it still makes me wonder why management did not let me go. Any other television station would have cut ties with an employee who had the potential to tarnish the wholesome image of the company. I had nothing to do with Mark's behavior—but I was still married to him. And that was bad enough. But WNEP-TV always placed its trust in me and believed that I would come out of this nightmare with my head held high. From the general managers to the newsroom supervisors to the production assistants—everyone offered me compassion, understanding, and support during those very dark days. They recognized how mortified I was when my name was dragged into news stories about Mark, and they knew how I desperately tried to save face as a public figure representing WNEP-TV. And yet the station still kept me on the air. I am so fortunate to say that I worked for a television station that was not just an employer, but an extended, caring family.

This book is written from the prospective I had of my two children as they were growing up and while they endured the emotional trauma of my husband's arrests. I refer to my child who we named Sarah as "she" in this book because that was the pronoun everyone used to describe Sarah at the time of the events described here. It has since been brought to my attention, that Sarah is nonbinary and has chosen to be referred to with the pronoun "they." Be assured, I wholeheartedly support and respect Sarah's, and anyone else's, decision to choose the gender, or lack of gender, that they identify with.

I am lucky to be the mother of two children who give me purpose every single day. Rachael and Sarah bring light into my life. My love for them is endless. I thank them with all my heart for giving me inspiration to write this book and for allowing me to tell our story of survival.

ABOUT THE AUTHOR

Marisa Burke owns Marisa Burke Communications, a multimedia agency operating in Colorado and Pennsylvania. A native of central Pennsylvania, Marisa is a graduate of the Roy H. Park School of Communications at Ithaca College, New York. She started her own business after a long broadcast journalism career at WNEP-TV, the top-rated ABC affiliate in Wilkes-Barre/Scranton, Pennsylvania, where she was main anchor and lead producer. Marisa received a national Edward R. Murrow award in 2005 and was awarded Broadcaster of the Year by the Pennsylvania Association of Broadcasters in 2017, not long after she concluded her local television news career.

NOTE FROM THE AUTHOR

Word-of-mouth is crucial for any author to succeed. If you enjoyed *Just Checking Scores*, please leave a review online—anywhere you are able. Even if it's just a sentence or two. It would make all the difference and would be very much appreciated.

Thanks!
Marisa Burke

We hope you enjoyed reading this title from:

BLACK ROSE
writing™

www.blackrosewriting.com

Subscribe to our mailing list – *The Rosevine* – and receive **FREE** books, daily deals, and stay current with news about upcoming releases and our hottest authors.
Scan the QR code below to sign up.

Already a subscriber? Please accept a sincere thank you for being a fan of Black Rose Writing authors.

View other Black Rose Writing titles at
www.blackrosewriting.com/books and use promo code
PRINT to receive a **20% discount** when purchasing..

Made in United States
North Haven, CT
29 July 2023